Contents

T0344041

Test type	Quantity	Total marks	Suggested timing	Pages
Introduction				4–5
Placement Test (A/B)	1	50	45 minutes	6–9
Vocabulary Checks (A/B)	8	20	15 minutes	10–25
Grammar Checks (A/B)	8	15	15 minutes	26–33
Language Tests (A/B): Vocabulary, Grammar, Communication	9	30	45 minutes	34–51
Skills Tests (A/B): Listening, Communication, Reading, Writing	4	30	45 minutes	52–67
Mid-Year Test 1–4 (A/B): Vocabulary, Grammar + Listening, Communication, Reading	1	30 + 20	45 + 35 minutes	68–71
End-of-Year Test 1–8 (A/B): Vocabulary, Grammar + Listening, Communication, Reading	1	30 + 20	45 + 35 minutes	72–75
Exam Tests 1–4: Reading & Writing, Listening & Communication	1	30	45 minutes	76–79
Exam Test 5–8: Reading & Writing, Listening & Communication	1	30	45 minutes	80–83
Speaking Tasks	4	20	5-8 minutes	84–87
Writing Tasks	8	10	10 minutes	88
Audio script				89–90
Answer key				91–95

GoGetter Tests

This booklet contains a complete tests package for *GoGetter* 2. All of the tests are in photocopiable format. Audio for the listening tasks is available for downloading from MyEnglishLab.

Assessment of learning or Assessment for learning?

GoGetter offers a variety of tests which enable the teacher to monitor students' progress both at acquiring the new language and developing language skills. Any test can be used either as an assessment of learning or an assessment for learning. Assessment of learning usually takes place after the learning has happened and provides information about what students have achieved by giving a mark or a grade. You can also use a test as an assessment for learning by providing specific feedback on students' strengths and weaknesses, and suggestions for improvement as part of the on-going learning process. A combination of both types of assessment can be a powerful tool for helping your students to learn.

It is very important to make sure students understand the tasks in every test and explain them if necessary. Also, it is very useful for students to receive constructive feedback and be advised how they can improve.

Versions of tests

Most tests have two versions: A and B. Versions A and B feature the same task types and are designed to have the same level of difficulty. However, the test items in each version are usually different or the sequence in which they occur differs. In the listening tasks, the test items are different but the audio is the same for both A and B versions, which makes it easy to administer a test.

You can use the tests that have two versions in two ways:

- give half the students in the class the A version and the other half the B version - this will help to deter students from cheating.
- give all students in the class the A version. You can then use the B version for students who missed the test or would like to retake it. Students who need a little more work on the unit objectives can use version B as remedial material.

Types of tests

Placement Test

The *GoGetter 2* Placement Test has been designed to help you decide which level of the *GoGetter* series, level 1, level 2 or level 3, is best suited to your students. If students score:

- 0-10 points (0-20%), we suggest they start at level 1.
- 11-20 points (21-39%), we suggest they start at level 2.
- 21-37 points (40-74%), you might consider an additional oral interview to decide whether level 2 or level 3 (the latter with some remedial work) would be more appropriate.
- 38-50 points (75+%), we suggest they start at level 3.

Vocabulary Checks

There are eight Vocabulary Checks. They test the key vocabulary sets taught in units 1-8 of the Students' Book. Each Vocabulary Check comprises three exercises. A Vocabulary Check can be administered upon completing all lessons with vocabulary input in a unit. Alternatively, it can be cut up into three mini-tests and administered after completing work on the relevant vocabulary set.

Grammar Checks

There are eight Grammar Checks. They test the grammar taught in lessons 2 and 3 of units 1-8 of the Students' Book. Each Grammar Check comprises three exercises. A Grammar Check can be administered upon completing lesson 3 of a unit. Alternatively, it can be cut up into two mini-tests and administered after completing work on the relevant grammar point.

Language Tests

There are nine Language Tests. They test the vocabulary, grammar and language for communication taught in the *Get started!* unit and units 1-8 of the Students' Book. The tests can be administered upon completing each unit.

Skills Tests

There are four Skills Tests. Each exploits the language taught in two successive units of the Students' Book. The Skills Tests check students' progress using the following skills-based tasks: Listening, Communication, Reading and Writing. In each test one of the listening tasks and the communication task mirror the exam-style tasks used in the relevant Skills Revision section in the Students' Book. The tests can be administered upon completing units 2, 4, 6 and 8.

Mid-Year Test and End-of-Year Test

The Mid-Year Test and the End-of-Year Test have the same structure and consist of two parts. The first part, Exercises 1-6, tests the vocabulary and grammar taught in the relevant units of the Students' Book. The second part, Exercises 7-9, is skills-based and comprises Listening, Communication and Reading. The Mid-Year Test should be administered after completing the first four units of the Students' Book, and the End-of-Year Test - after all units have been completed.

Exam Tests

There are two Exam Tests. Exam Test 1-4 should be used after completing the first four units of the Students' Book including *Skills Revision*. Exam Test 5-8 should be administered after units 5-8 have been completed. The two tests mirror the Exam Practice section of the *GoGetter 2 Workbook* and comprise two sections: Reading & Writing and Listening & Communication. These tests provide the opportunity to check students' progress and proficiency through typical exam tasks similar to those in *Pearson Test of English for Young Learners* and *Cambridge English: Young Learners of English Tests* (adapted to suit this level and age group).

Speaking Tasks

There are four sets of Speaking Tasks, each enabling you to test the material from two successive units. Each set has visual material for the student and notes for the teacher at the bottom of the page, which should be cut off along the dotted line. There are two tasks in the notes for the teacher:

- Task 1: elicitation of the vocabulary illustrated,
- Task 2: asking and answering personalised questions related to both the picture and the student's experience.

The student should respond using structures and vocabulary from the relevant units.

The Speaking Tasks can complement the respective Skills Tests, Mid-Year Test and End-of-Year Test or be administered separately. The following marking criteria and evaluation scales will help you mark consistently and give students meaningful feedback.

Marking criteria

- 0–5 points for the range of language used (structures and vocabulary). See the list of target structures and vocabulary for each Speaking Task in the notes for the teacher.
- 0–5 points for accuracy of expression
- 0–5 points for fluency
- 0–5 points for pronunciation

Evaluation scales	Language range	Accuracy	Fluency	Pronunciation
Excellent 18–20 points	The student commands a full range of the vocabulary and grammar taught and uses it appropriately.	The student makes no or very few mistakes.	The student speaks fluently, with no hesitation. He/She can use full sentences. Students should not be penalised for using single words or phrases where appropriate.	The student's pronunciation is clear and accurate.
Good 15–17 points	The student commands a good range of the vocabulary and grammar taught.	The student makes mistakes occasionally.	The student speaks fluently, with little hesitation. He/She can use full sentences. Students should not be penalised for using single words or phrases where appropriate.	The student's pronunciation is clear and accurate most of the time.
Satisfactory 10–14 points	The student can use some of the basic vocabulary and grammar taught.	The student makes mistakes but these do not prevent communication.	The student speaks with some hesitation because he/she is trying to think of the right words. He/She answers using full sentences some of the time but clearly prefers using phrases.	The student's pronunciation is clear on the whole; occasional poor pronunciation does not prevent communication.
Unsatisfactory 6–9 points	The student can use very little vocabulary and grammar.	The student makes a lot of mistakes which hinder good communication. He/She is able to communicate successfully at least once.	The student hesitates frequently because he/she cannot think of the right words. He/She answers using mainly phrases or single words.	The student's pronunciation is poor and makes communication difficult.
Very poor 0–5 points	The student gives no answer or knows only a few basic words.	The student is unable to communicate or gives inaccurate answers that prevent communication.	The student cannot think of the right words and says very little.	The student gives no answer or can pronounce fairly correctly only a few words.

Writing Tasks

There are eight Writing Tasks corresponding to Units 1–8 in the Students' Book. You can use the tasks as in-class writing tests or assign them as homework.

Each writing task contains a topic, several questions that students are asked to refer to in their works and a word limit. The tasks for all units have a 60–70-word limit.

The following marking criteria and evaluation scales are provided to help you mark consistently and to give students meaningful feedback.

Marking criteria

- 0–5 points for content. Award 5 marks if the student refers to at least 5 questions / gives 5 different pieces of information connected with the topic.
- 1 point for not going under or over the word limit
- 2 points for accuracy of expression
- 2 points for the range of language used. See the Marking check lists and model texts for each writing task on page 95 of this booklet.

Evaluation scales

Excellent:	9–10 points
Good:	7–8 points
Satisfactory:	5–6 points
Unsatisfactory:	3–4 points
Very poor:	0–2 points

Tests on MyEnglishLab

Visit www.MyEnglishLab.com to access the following:

- online versions of Skills tests, Mid-Year Test and End-of-Year Test, which can be assigned to your students and automatically checked,
- *GoGetter Tests* in PDF and editable format, and audio for tests,
- PDF versions of *GoGetter Tests* adjusted to the needs of dyslectic students.

Use the Teacher Access Code to unlock the teacher content on MyEnglishLab. You will find the code and registration details in *GoGetter* Teacher's Book.

Placement Test A

name ______________________ class ______

Vocabulary

1 Circle the odd one out.

0	wardrobe	sofa	shelves	(jumper)
1	March	Art	Science	P.E.
2	worried	scared	excited	bored
3	canteen	kitchen	gym	playground
4	bread	cheese	milk	meat
5	chef	hall	pilot	vet

[ ] / [5]

2 Label the pictures.

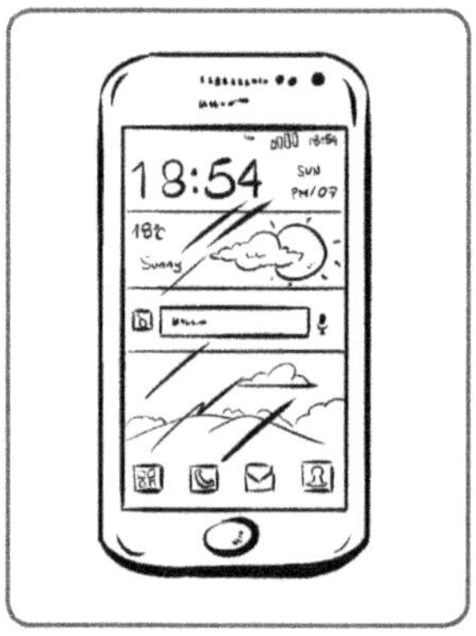

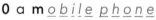

0 a m*obile phone*

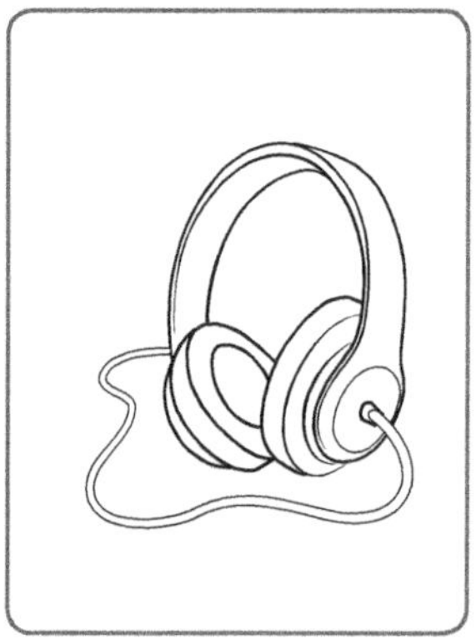

1 h _ _ _ _ _ _ _ _ _

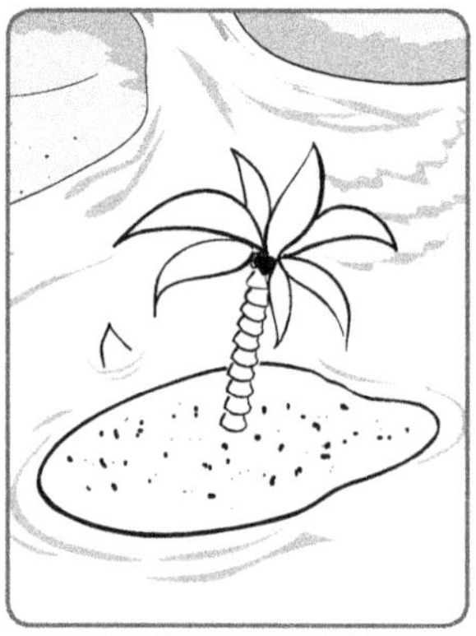

2 an i _ _ _ _ _

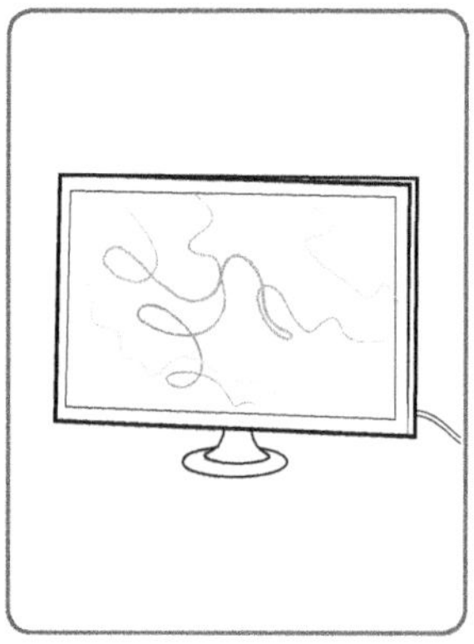

3 a s _ _ _ _ _

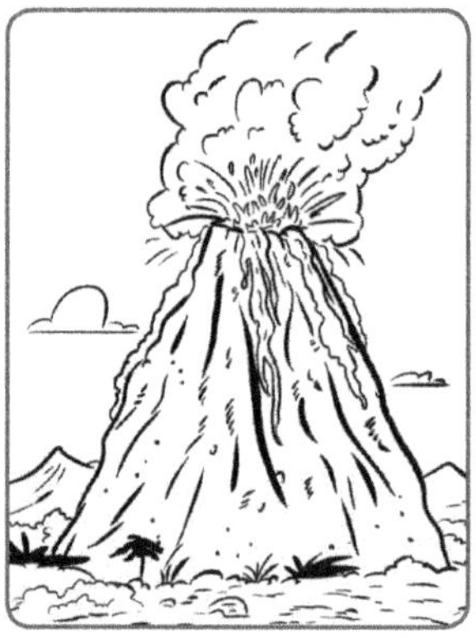

4 a v _ _ _ _ _ _

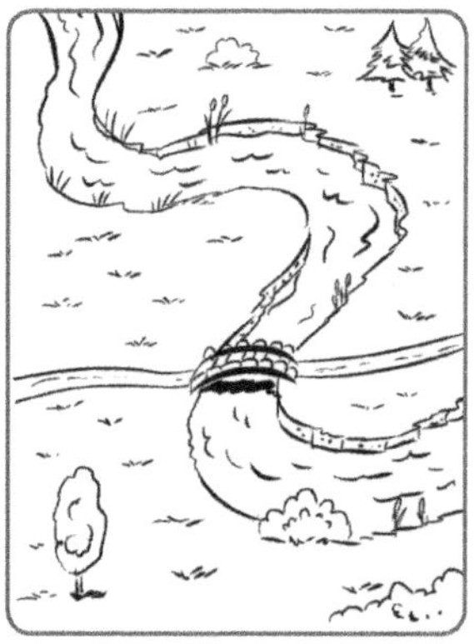

5 a r _ _ _ _

[ ] / [5]

3 Circle the correct word.

0 Do you walk to school or do you *run* / (*ride*) / *go* a bike?

1 I don't buy CDs. I *download* / *surf* / *text* songs from the Internet.

2 Mum and Dad *make* / *take* / *do* the shopping every weekend at the supermarket.

3 We *live* / *leave* / *go* home at half past seven and arrive at school at eight.

4 You can *buy* / *visit* / *look* some great souvenirs in this shop.

5 Are you going to *see* / *stay* / *get* in a hotel or go camping?

[ ] / [5]

4 Complete the text with the words in the box.

about ~~classical~~ expensive get opposite restaurant

On 24th November there's a concert of [0]*classical* music in town. We're going to take the tram and we're going to [1]__________ off at the stop [2]__________ the theatre. The tickets aren't [3]__________, they're only 2 pounds! After the concert, we're going to have dinner at the [4]__________ between the library and the museum. I'm very excited [5]__________ it.

[ ] / [5]

Grammar

5 Circle the correct word.

0 Boris is *a* / (*an*) / *some* artist and he paints beautiful pictures.

1 How *much* / *many* / *any* butter is there in the fridge?

2 The ham sandwiches are *good* / *better* / *best* than the tuna sandwiches.

3 *I am usually* / *I never am* / *I always am* late for school.

4 There aren't *a* / *some* / *any* people in the park this evening.

5 What are *more intelligent* / *the intelligent* / *the most intelligent* animals in the world?

[ ] / [5]

Placement Test A

name ______________________ class ________

6 **Use the Present Simple or Present Continuous form of the verbs.**

0 Polly *practises* (practise) the guitar every afternoon after school.
1 The student ______________ (study) for her English exam at the moment.
2 We speak French but we ______________ (not speak) Spanish.
3 I ______________ (not watch) TV in the living room now.
4 Sam ______________ (not brush) his teeth after meals so he has bad teeth!
5 My family and I ______________ (always / go) on holiday to the mountains.

[ ] / [5]

7 **Use the Past Simple form of the verbs.**

HOME | ABOUT ME | CONTACT

I usually walk to school but last Friday I [0] *cycled* (cycle) there. I [1] ______________ (have) lessons from half past eight to three o'clock. In the afternoon, my friends and I [2] ______________ (play) basketball. Then I [3] ______________ (go) home. I [4] ______________ (feel) tired so I [5] ______________ (not meet) my friends in the evening.

[ ] / [5]

8 **Use the words in the box to complete the dialogues.**

are did ~~don't~~ going is were

A: Do you get up early every morning?
B: No, I [0] *don't*. I get up late at the weekend.

A: What [1] __________ you and your brother doing right now?
B: I'm having breakfast but my brother [2] __________ sleeping!

A: Where [3] __________ you yesterday?
B: We visited my grandparents in London.

A: [4] __________ you watch the film on TV last night?
B: Yes, it was great!

A: What are you [5] __________ to do tomorrow?
B: I'm not sure.

[ ] / [5]

Communication

9 **Match questions 1–5 with answers a–f. There is one extra answer.**

0 How do you spell your name? [g]
1 What's your phone number? [ ]
2 Would you like anything to eat? [ ]
3 Can I speak to Yvonne, please? [ ]
4 What do you think of cartoons? [ ]
5 What's your favourite book? [ ]

a No, thanks. I'm fine.
b 998112.
c *Harry Potter and the Philosopher's Stone.*
d I'm afraid she's out.
e In my opinion, they're silly.
f Yes, that's fine.
g H-A-N-N-A-H.

[ ] / [5]

10 **Complete the dialogues with the words in the box. There is one extra word.**

~~busy~~ can do here like sounds sure

A: Are you [0] *busy* next Saturday? I've got tickets for a football match.
B: That [1] __________ great. I'd love to come.

A: I'd [2] __________ a ticket to London, please.
B: [3] __________ you are.

A: [4] __________ I borrow a pen, please?
B: [5] __________, no problem.

[ ] / [5]

Vocabulary	[ ] / [20]	Communication	[ ] / [10]
Grammar	[ ] / [20]	**Your total score**	[ ] / [50]

© Pearson Education Limited 2017 PHOTOCOPIABLE

Placement Test B

name _____   class _____

Vocabulary

1 Circle the odd one out.

0 wardrobe	sofa	shelves	(jumper)
1 April	Maths	History	Geography
2 potato	rice	meat	salad
3 tired	bored	interested	worried
4 builder	canteen	nurse	police officer
5 staff room	garden	library	hall

☐ / 5

2 Label the pictures.

0 a m _o b i l e_ _p h o n e_

1 a s _ _ _ _ _

2 a r _ _ _ _ _

3 an i _ _ _ _ _ _

4 h _ _ _ _ _ _ _ _

5 a v _ _ _ _ _ _

☐ / 5

3 Circle the correct word.

0 Do you walk to school or do you *run /*(*ride*)*/ go* a bike?

1 The students leave home at quarter to eight and *arrive / go / get on* at school at eight.

2 Let's *do / go / have* sightseeing in the city tomorrow.

3 I *make / take / empty* the bin every night before I go to bed.

4 How often do you *download / text / surf* your friends?

5 Dad loves *taking / making / looking* photos with his new camera.

☐ / 5

4 Complete the text with the words in the box.

> between   cheap   ~~classical~~   excited
> opposite   take

On 3rd December there's a concert of **0**_classical_ music in town. I'm very **1**_____ about it. We're going to **2**_____ the bus and get off at the stop **3**_____ the theatre. The tickets are **4**_____. They are only 2 pounds! After the concert, we're going to have dinner at the café **5**_____ the library and the museum.

☐ / 5

Grammar

5 Circle the correct word.

0 Boris is *a /*(*an*)*/ some* artist and he paints beautiful pictures.

1 We *sometimes eat / eat often / eat usually* pizza at the weekend.

2 What is *the difficult / more difficult / the most difficult* language in the world?

3 How *any / many / much* sugar do you want in your coffee?

4 There are *a / some / any* interesting programmes on TV tonight.

5 The first song was *bad / worse / worst* than the second song.

☐ / 5

Placement Test B

________________________ name ________ class

6 **Use the Present Simple or Present Continuous form of the verbs.**

0 Polly _practises_ (practise) the guitar every afternoon after school.
1 I __________ (not listen) to music right now.
2 Denise and Rob __________ (usually / go) to the beach in summer.
3 I speak Polish but I __________ (not speak) French.
4 Mum __________ (wash) her car every week.
5 Greg __________ (do) his homework at the moment.

[ ] / [5]

7 **Use the Past Simple form of the verbs.**

HOME | ABOUT ME | CONTACT

I usually cycle to town at the weekend but last Saturday I [0]_walked_ (walk) there. I [1]__________ (meet) my friends at the shopping centre and I [2]__________ (buy) some jeans. In the afternoon, we [3]__________ (watch) a football match at the stadium. After that I [4]__________ (feel) tired so I [5]__________ (not go) to a café with my friends.

[ ] / [5]

8 **Use the words in the box to complete the dialogues.**

are did ~~don't~~ going is was

A: What time [0]_do_ you get up in the morning?
B: At seven o'clock.

A: How many hours [1]________ you study last night?
B: Two hours.

A: What are they [2]________ to do tomorrow?
B: I'm not sure.

A: What [3]________ you and your sister doing right now?
B: My sister [4]________ washing the dishes and I'm helping her.

A: Where [5]________ James yesterday?
B: He visited his cousins in London.

[ ] / [5]

Communication

9 **Match questions 1–5 with answers a–f. There is one extra answer.**

0 How do you spell your name? [g]
1 Can I speak to Fred, please? [ ]
2 What's your favourite sport? [ ]
3 What do you think of these computer games? [ ]
4 Would you like anything to drink? [ ]
5 What's your email address? [ ]

a I'd like some orange juice.
b In my opinion, they're cool.
c Windsurfing.
d julietmorris@ffmc.com
e No, sorry, it isn't OK.
f Just a minute.
g P-R-U-D-E-N-C-E.

[ ] / [5]

10 **Complete the dialogues with the words in the box. There is one extra word.**

borrow excuse problem sounds straight right ~~would~~

A: I've got tickets for a basketball match on Wednesday. [0]_Would_ you like to come with me?
B: That [1]________ great. I'd love to come.

A: Can I [2]________ your dictionary, please?
B: Sure, no [3]________.

A: [4]________ me. How can I get to Oxford Street?
B: Go [5]________ on. Then turn right.

[ ] / [5]

Vocabulary	[ ] / [20]	Communication	[ ] / [10]
Grammar	[ ] / [20]	**Your total score**	[ ] / [50]

© Pearson Education Limited 2017 PHOTOCOPIABLE

1 Vocabulary Check A

name ____________________ class ______

1.1 School A

1 Complete the sentences with the words in the box.

~~Art~~ calculator dictionary French Geography History map Music Science scissors trainers

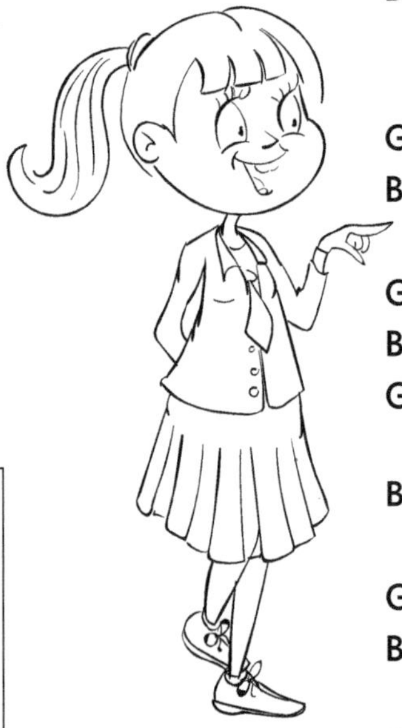

Girl: My favourite subject is [0]*Art*. I love drawing and painting.
Boy: And [1] __________ is *my* favourite subject. I like learning about the past.

Girl: I love learning [2] __________. What's *'Vouloir, c'est pouvoir'* in English?
Boy: I don't know, but I can use my [3] __________ to find the words!

Girl: In [4] __________ lessons we sing and play the guitar or piano.
Boy: In [5] __________ lessons we do cool experiments!
Girl: In [6] __________ we learn about different countries. Look at this [7] __________ of Poland. Can you find Warsaw on it?
Boy: Yes, there it is!

Girl: Have you got [8] __________ and a ruler in your pencil case?
Boy: Yes, I have. We have Maths at half past eight. I need my [9] __________!
Girl: We have P.E. today. Where are my [10] __________? I can't find them!

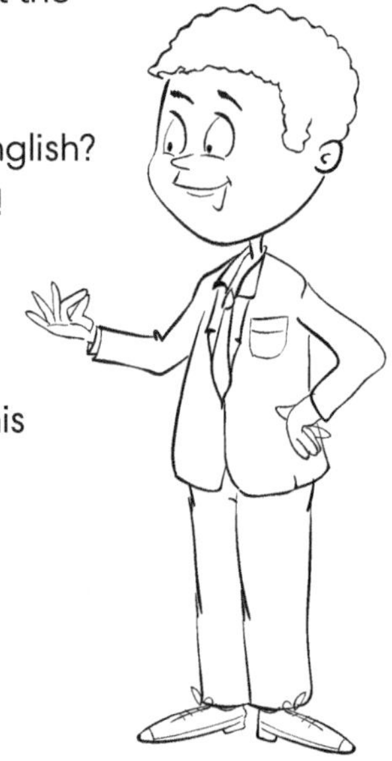

☐ / 10

name ____________________ class ______

1.3 *Do, play* A

2 Circle the correct word.

0 Gina *does* / *plays* tennis every weekend.
1 Janice *does* / *plays* ballet on Monday afternoon.
2 I *do* / *play* karate on Saturdays.
3 Ben *does* / *plays* basketball for the school team.
4 Oliver and Ian have the same hobby. They *do* / *play* pottery.
5 Lisa *does* / *plays* chess well. She's the school champion!

☐ / 5

name ____________________ class ______

1.5 Places in a school A

3 Match sentences 1–5 with places a–e.

0 We have lessons in this room. [f]
1 We have lunch in this place. ☐
2 The teachers relax and work in this room. ☐
3 There are books, DVDs, CDs and computers in this room. ☐
4 We play and talk to our friends in this place. ☐
5 There are lots of laptops in this room. ☐

a canteen
b playground
c computer room
d library
e staff room
f classroom

☐ / 5

Your total score ☐ / 20

1 Vocabulary Check B

name ______________________ class ______

1.1 School **B**

1 Complete the sentences with the words in the box.

~~Art~~ calculator dictionary French Geography History map Music ruler Science trainers

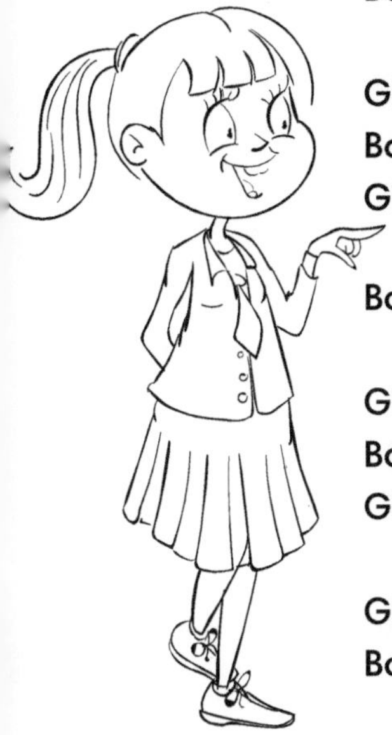

Girl: My favourite subject is 0 *Art*. I love drawing and painting.
Boy: And *my* favourite subject is 1 ________. I love learning about the past.

Girl: We sing and play the piano in 2 ________ lessons.
Boy: We do cool experiments in 3 ________ lessons!
Girl: We learn about different countries in 4 ________ lessons.
Can you find Liverpool on this 5 ________ of the UK?
Boy: Yes, there it is!

Girl: Is there a 6 ________ and a rubber in your pencil case?
Boy: Yes, there is. We have Maths at ten. I need my 7 ________!
Girl: We have P.E. today. Where are my 8 ________? I can't find them!

Girl: I love learning 9 ________. What's *'Vouloir, c'est pouvoir' in English?*
Boy: I don't know, but I can use my 10 ________ to find the words!

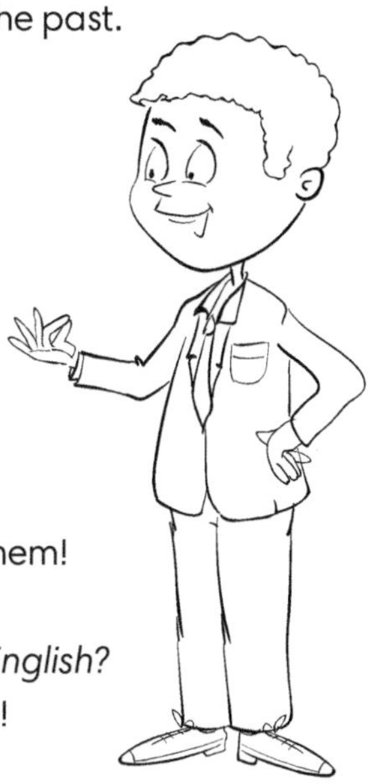

☐ / 10

name ______________________ class ______

1.3 *Do, play* **B**

2 Circle the correct word.

0 Gina *does* / *plays* tennis every weekend.
1 Harry and Nina love *doing* / *playing* basketball.
2 I *do* / *play* ballet on Tuesday and Thursday afternoon.
3 Megan *does* / *plays* pottery. She makes lot of cool things.
4 Sam and I have the same hobby. We *do* / *play* chess.
5 Lucy *does* / *plays* judo on Saturdays.

☐ / 5

name ______________________ class ______

1.5 Places in a school **B**

3 Match sentences 1–5 with places a–e.

0 We have lessons in this room. [f]
1 We run, jump and do exercise in this place. ☐
2 We have lunch in this place. ☐
3 The teachers relax and work in this room. ☐
4 The teachers and students meet in this place every morning. ☐
5 There are books, DVDs, CDs and computers in this room. ☐

a canteen
b gym
c hall
d library
e staff room
f classroom

☐ / 5

Your total score ☐ / 20

name _____   class _____

2.1 Food and drink (1)

1 Look at the picture and complete the text.

My food

I usually eat an ⁰a*pple*, ¹c_____ and
²y_____ for breakfast. I drink a glass
of ³o_____ j_____ too. At one
o'clock, I eat some ⁴b_____,
⁵c_____ and two or three ⁶b_____.
In the evening, I eat dinner with my family.
We often have ⁷c_____ and ⁸v_____
or ⁹s_____ and ¹⁰t_____.

A

☐ / 10

---

name _____   class _____

2.2 Food and drink (2)

A

2 Match sentences 1–5 with food a–e.

0 Chickens make them. They're white and yellow inside.   [f]
1 It's yellow and you put it on bread.   ☐
2 It's a small red fruit.   ☐
3 It's a small yellow fruit.   ☐
4 It's dark brown. Children usually love eating it.   ☐
5 You make bread with it.   ☐

a butter
b chocolate
c strawberry
d flour
e lemon
f eggs

☐ / 5

---

name _____   class _____

2.3 Containers

A

3 Complete the shopping list with the words in the box.

bar ~~bottle~~ can carton jar packet

Shopping list

0 a *bottle* of water
1 a _____ of juice
2 a _____ of chocolate
3 a _____ of biscuits
4 a _____ of jam
5 a _____ of cola

☐ / 5

Your total score ☐ / 20

2 Vocabulary Check B

name ______________ class ____

2.1 Food and drink (1)

B

1 Look at the picture and complete the text.

My food

I usually eat an ⁰a*pple*, ¹b__________ and ²c__________ for breakfast. At one o'clock, I eat some ³f__________ and two ⁴b__________. In the afternoon, I eat ⁵y__________ or ⁶c__________. In the evening, I have dinner with my family. We sometimes have ⁷m__________ and ⁸p__________ or ⁹c__________ with ¹⁰v__________.

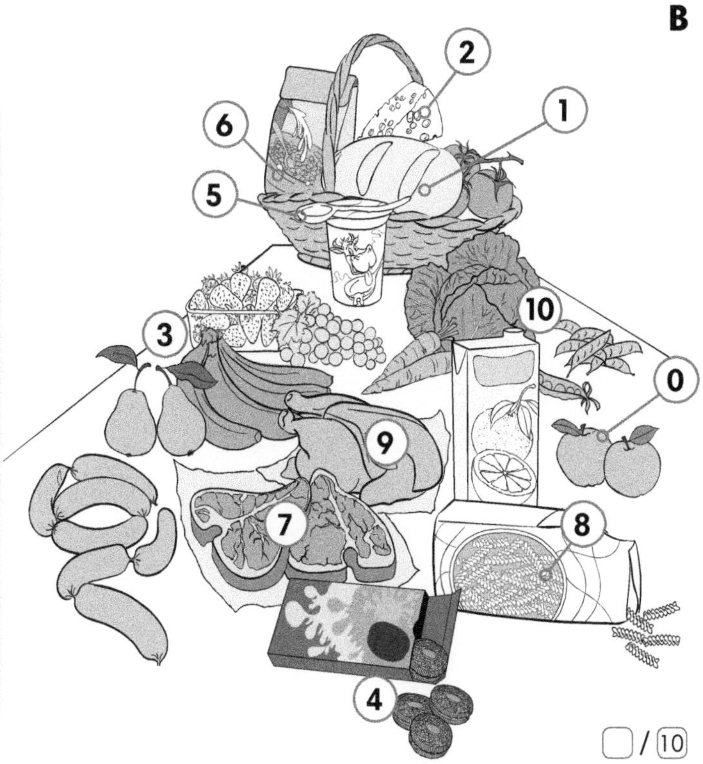

☐ / [10]

name ______________ class ____

2.2 Food and drink (2)

B

2 Match sentences 1–5 with food a–e.

0 Chickens make them. They're white and yellow inside. [*f*]
1 It's a yellow fruit. ☐
2 We make cakes and bread with it. ☐
3 You put it on bread. It's yellow. ☐
4 It's a small red fruit. ☐
5 Children usually love eating it. It's brown. ☐

a flour
b lemon
c butter
d chocolate
e strawberry
f eggs

☐ / [5]

name ______________ class ____

2.3 Containers

B

3 Complete the shopping list with the words in the box.

bar ~~bottle~~ can carton jar packet

Shopping list

0 a *bottle* of water
1 a __________ of jam
2 a __________ of cola
3 a __________ of chocolate
4 a __________ of juice
5 a __________ of biscuits

☐ / [5]

Your total score ☐ / [20]

3 Vocabulary Check A

name ______________________ class ______

3.1 Technology **A**

1 Look at the pictures and write the words. There is one extra word/phrase.

download a song   headphones   keyboard   mouse   ~~printer~~   screen   send an email   speakers   surf the Internet   take a selfie   talk on the phone   text a friend

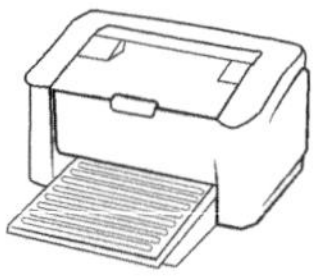

0 *printer*

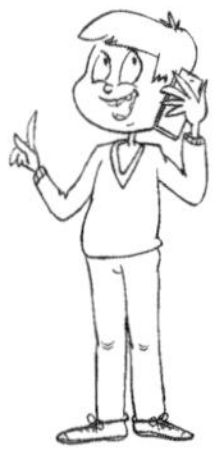

1 ______________

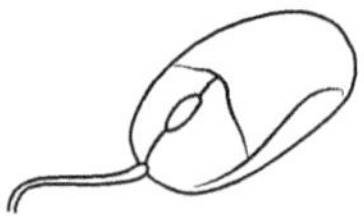

2 ______________

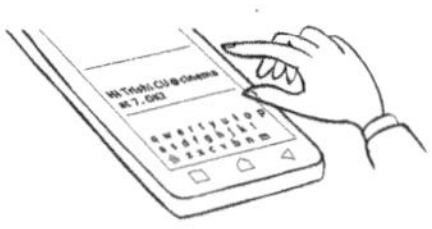

3 ______________

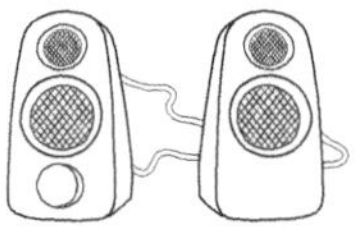

4 ______________

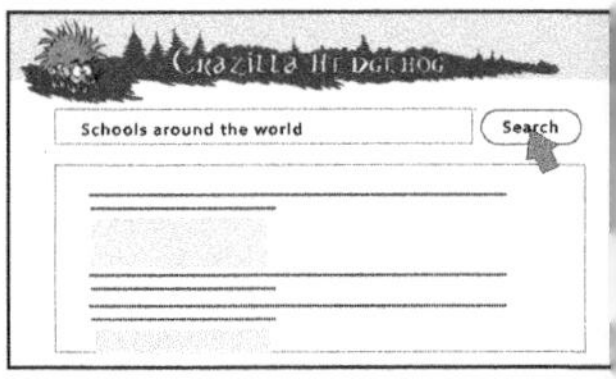

5 ______________

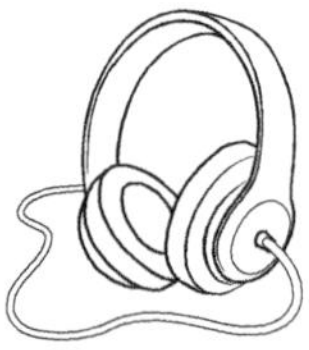

6 ______________

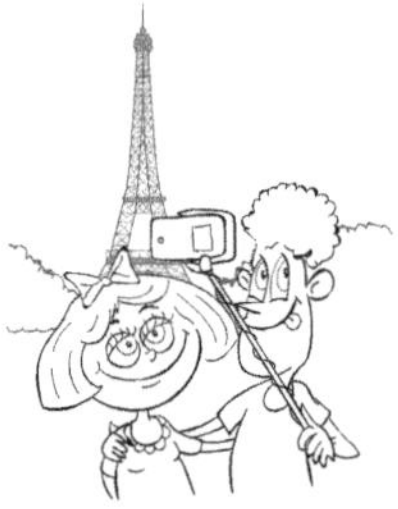

7 ______________

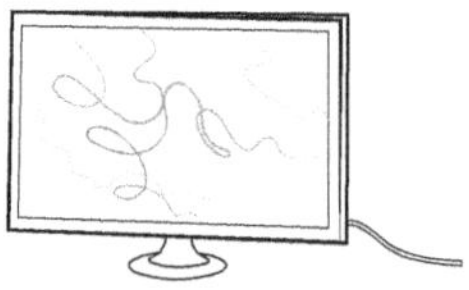

8 ______________

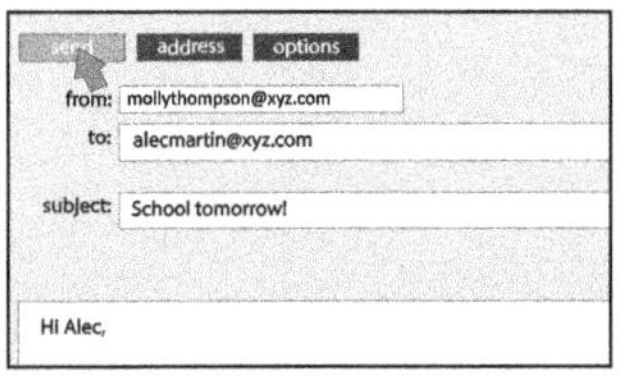

9 ______________

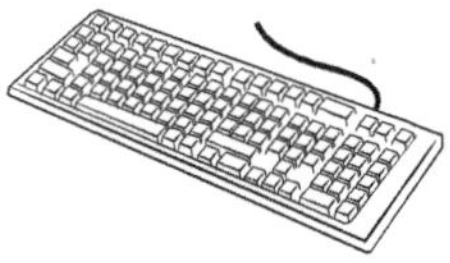

10 ______________

☐ / 10

name ______________________ class ______

3.3 Feelings **A**

2 Look at the faces and complete the sentences with the correct adjectives.

0 I have a new puppy and I'm **h***appy*! 

1 Dad works a lot and he feels **t**__________. 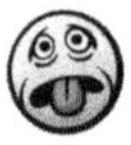

2 Every day is the same. I'm **b**__________. 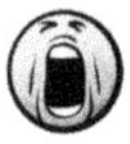

3 Mum is late and I'm **w**__________. What's wrong? 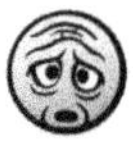

4 They don't like me. I feel **s**__________. 

5 He uses my computer but he doesn't ask me. I'm **a**__________. 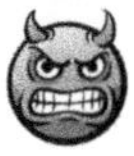

☐ / 5

name ______________________ class ______

3.5 Adjectives with prepositions **A**

3 Complete the sentences. Use *about*, *at*, *in* or *of*.

0 Fred is good *at* tennis. He's the school champion.

1 What's the matter? I'm worried ________ you.

2 We're interested ________ science and technology.

3 I'm excited ______ my birthday party on Saturday.

4 Are you scared ________ spiders?

5 They can't play chess well. They're bad ________ it.

☐ / 5

Your total score ☐ / 20

3 Vocabulary Check B

name ______________________ class ________

3.1 Technology

B

1 Look at the pictures and write the words. There is one extra word/phrase.

download a song · headphones · keyboard · mouse · ~~printer~~ · screen · send an email · speakers · surf the Internet · take a selfie · talk on the phone · text a friend

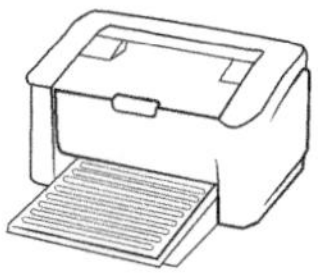

0 *printer*

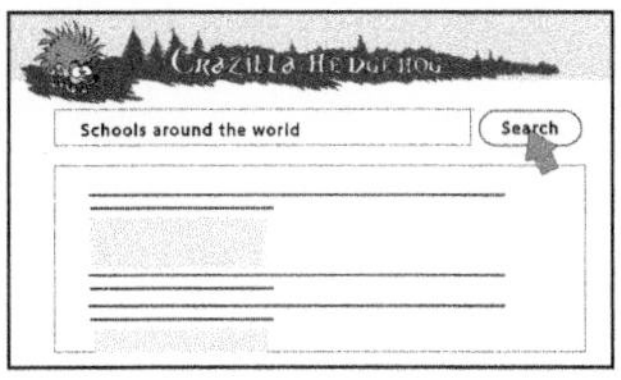

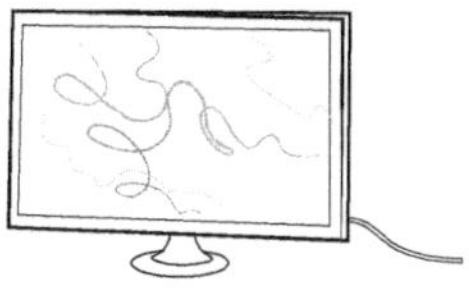

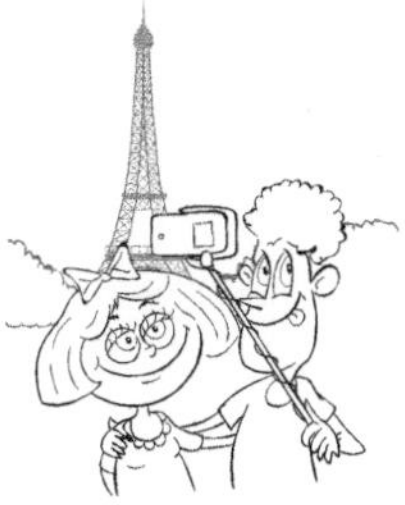

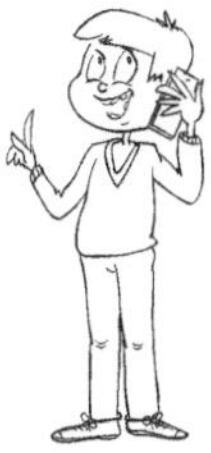

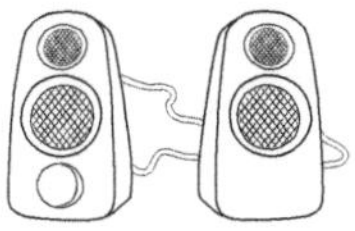

1 ____________ 2 ____________ 3 ____________ 4 ____________ 5 ____________

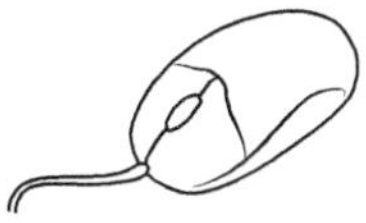

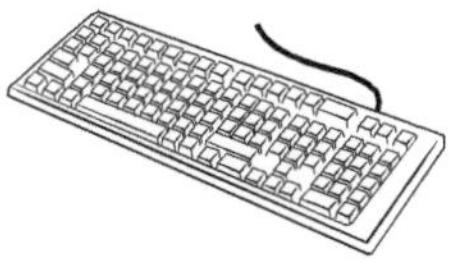

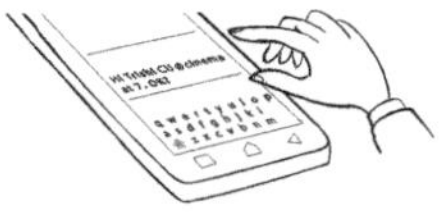

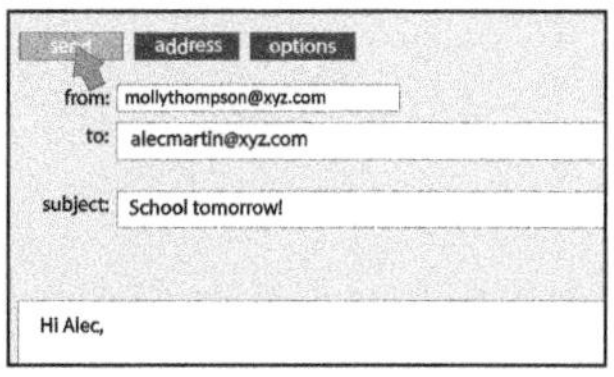

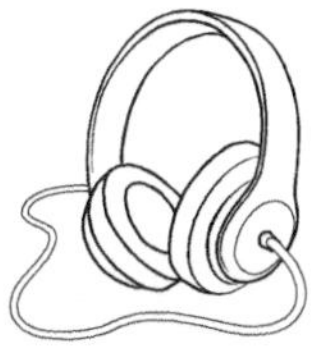

6 ____________ 7 ____________ 8 ____________ 9 ____________ 10 ____________

[ ] / [10]

---

name ______________________ class ________

3.3 Feelings

B

2 Look at the faces and complete the sentences with the correct adjectives.

0 I have a new puppy and I'm h*appy*! 

1 The little girl can't find her mother. She's s__________. 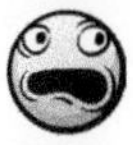

2 Dad is late and I'm w__________. What's wrong? 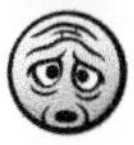

3 My parents work a lot and they feel t__________ in the evening. 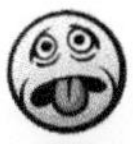

4 He doesn't like me and I feel s__________. 

5 Every day is the same and she's b__________. 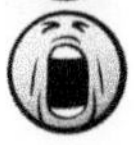

[ ] / [5]

---

name ______________________ class ________

3.5 Adjectives with prepositions

B

3 Complete the sentences. Use *about*, *at*, *in* or *of*.

0 Fred is good *at* tennis. He's the school champion.

1 She's excited ________ her birthday party on Friday.

2 I can't play chess. I'm bad ________ it.

3 They're interested ________ history and science.

4 Why are you scared ________ snakes?

5 I'm worried ________ you. What's the matter?

[ ] / [5]

Your total score [ ] / [20]

4 Vocabulary Check A

name ______________________ class ______

4.1 Geographical features **A**

1 Look at the picture and write the words. There is one extra word.

beach city desert forest island lake
~~mountain~~ river sea town volcano waterfall

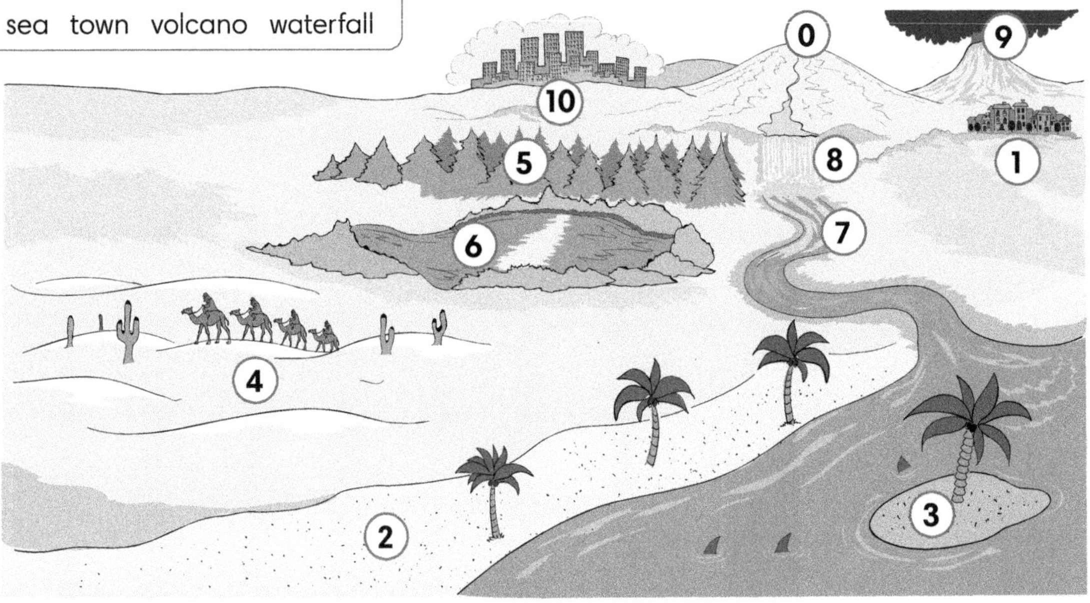

0 *mountain*
1 ______
2 ______
3 ______
4 ______
5 ______
6 ______
7 ______
8 ______
9 ______
10 ______

☐ / 10

name ______________________ class ______

4.2 Adjectives (1) **A**

2 Look at the adjectives in bold. Use adjectives with the opposite meaning.

0 I'm going for a **short** walk today. I don't want to go for a **l***ong* walk.
1 Don't go swimming in the sea. It isn't **s**__________. It's **dangerous**.
2 I love that film! It isn't **boring**. It's **e**__________.
3 Mount Everest is a very **high** mountain. That mountain over there is **l**__________.
4 I want a **c**__________ laptop. That laptop is too **expensive**.
5 I can do this **easy** exercise but I can't do that **d**__________ exercise.

☐ / 5

name ______________________ class ______

4.4 Adjectives (2) **A**

3 Match sentences 1–5 with sentences a–e.

0 She's got a lot of friends. Everyone likes her. [*f*]
1 She does a lot of exercise and she can work a lot too. ☐
2 She doesn't like it when people are sad. She's always nice to everyone. ☐
3 She's got great hair and a great face. People like looking at her. ☐
4 She tells good jokes. ☐
5 She's got fantastic marks at school and she's good at Maths and Science. ☐

a She's funny.
b She's kind.
c She's intelligent.
d She's beautiful.
e She's strong.
f She's friendly.

☐ / 5

Your total score ☐ / 20

4 Vocabulary Check B

name ______________________ class ______

4.1 Geographical features **B**

1 Look at the picture and write the words. There is one extra word.

beach city desert forest island lake ~~mountain~~ river sea town volcano waterfall

0 *mountain*
1 ______
2 ______
3 ______
4 ______
5 ______
6 ______
7 ______
8 ______
9 ______
10 ______

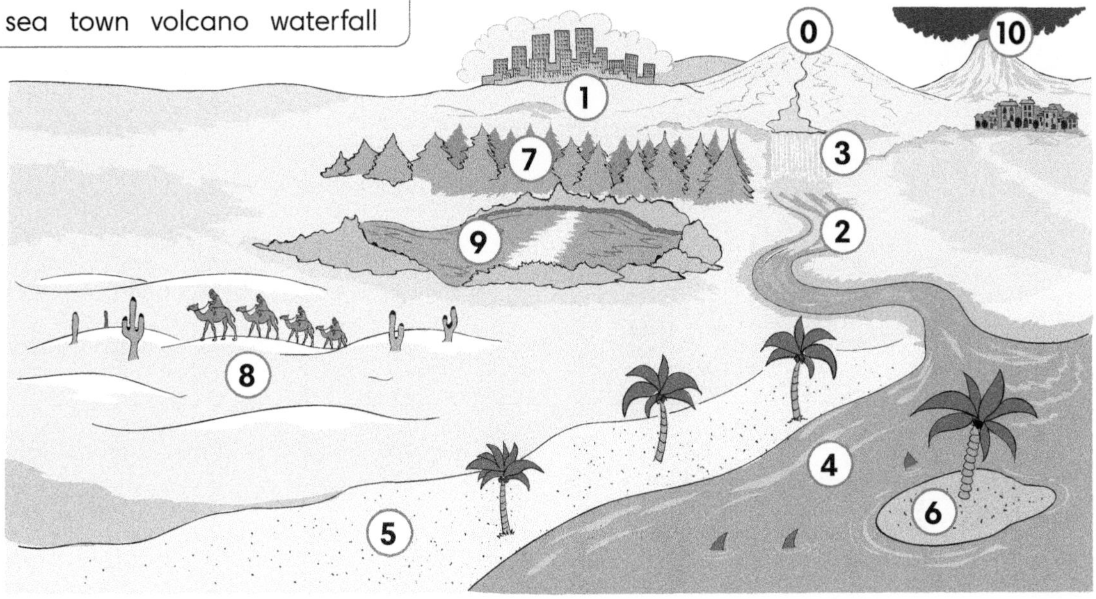

/ 10

name ______________________ class ______

4.2 Adjectives (1) **B**

2 Look at the adjectives in bold. Use adjectives with the opposite meaning.

0 I'm going for a **short** walk today. I don't want to go for a **l***ong* walk.
1 This mountain is **low**. Mont Blanc is a **h**______ mountain.
2 They can do the **e**______ exercises but they can't do the **difficult** exercises.
3 I want a **cheap** phone. This mobile phone is too **e**______.
4 Don't go sailing in this bad weather. It isn't **s**______. It's **dangerous**.
5 That DVD isn't **boring**. I love it! It's **e**______.

/ 5

name ______________________ class ______

4.4 Adjectives (2) **B**

3 Match sentences 1–5 with sentences a–e.

0 She's got a lot of friends. Everyone likes her. [*f*]
1 She's got fantastic marks at school and she's good at Science and Maths. [ ]
2 She's got great hair and a great face. People like looking at her. [ ]
3 She does a lot of exercise and she can work a lot. [ ]
4 She's good at running and she's a champion athlete. [ ]
5 She doesn't want people to be sad. She's nice to everyone. [ ]

a She's kind.
b She's beautiful.
c She's fast.
d She's strong.
e She's intelligent.
f She's friendly.

/ 5

Your total score / 20

© Pearson Education Limited 2017 PHOTOCOPIABLE

5 Vocabulary Check A

name ______________________ class ______

5.1 Places in town (1), prepositions of place — A

1 Look at the map and complete the text with the words in the box.

behind	between	café	hospital	in front of	library	museum	opposite	~~park~~	restaurant	stadium

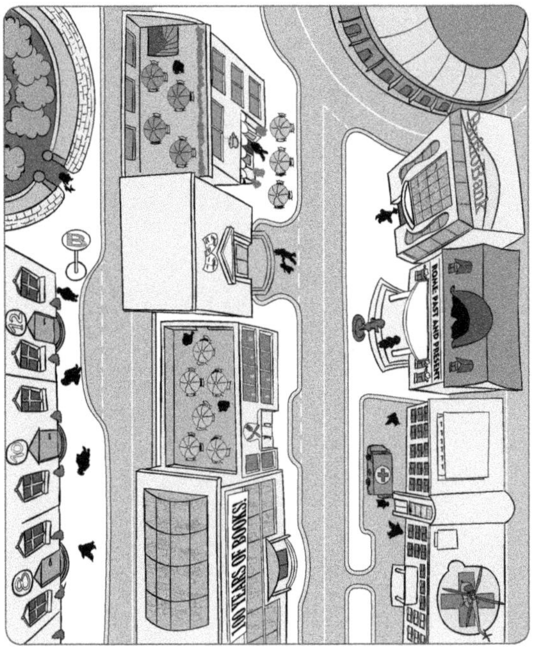

I live at 12 Albion Way. There's a small [0]*park* in my street. The bus stop is [1] __________ my house. The history [2] __________ is in Alexander Avenue. It's [3] __________ the bank and the [4] __________. My mum's a doctor there. The new football [5] __________ is in Alexander Avenue too. The Royal Theatre is [6] __________ the bank. I never go there but my friends and I sometimes have ice cream at the [7] __________ next to the theatre. And my parents love having dinner at the [8] __________ next to the theatre. My favourite building in the city is the [9] __________. It's got thousands of great books. My best friend's house is in my street, [10] __________ the library.

☐ / 10

name ______________________ class ______

5.4 Places in town (2) — A

2 Match beginnings 1–5 with endings a–e.

0 I play volleyball at the sports [*f*]
1 Please meet me at the swimming ☐
2 I meet my friends at the shopping ☐
3 There isn't a police ☐
4 The people at the train ☐
5 The post ☐

a station in our town.
b pool this afternoon.
c office is next to the bank.
d centre and we hang out.
e station are waiting for their train.
f centre after school.

☐ / 5

name ______________________ class ______

5.6 Adjectives — A

3 Look at the adjectives in bold. Use adjectives with the opposite meaning.

0 The forest isn't a **safe** place. There are a lot of *d a n g e r o u s* animals there.
1 I don't live in a _ _ _ city. I live in a **small** town.
2 The kitchen is _ _ _ _ _ but the bathroom is **clean**.
3 I don't like **old** houses. I like _ _ _ _ _ _ houses.
4 The Science Museum is **interesting** but the History Museum is _ _ _ _ _ _.
5 On Saturday night the streets are _ _ _ _ but they are **quiet** on Sunday morning.

☐ / 5

Your total score ☐ / 20

5 Vocabulary Check B

name ______________________ class ______

5.1 Places in town (1), prepositions of place **B**

1 Look at the map and complete the text with the words in the box.

behind between café hospital in front of library museum opposite ~~park~~ restaurant stadium

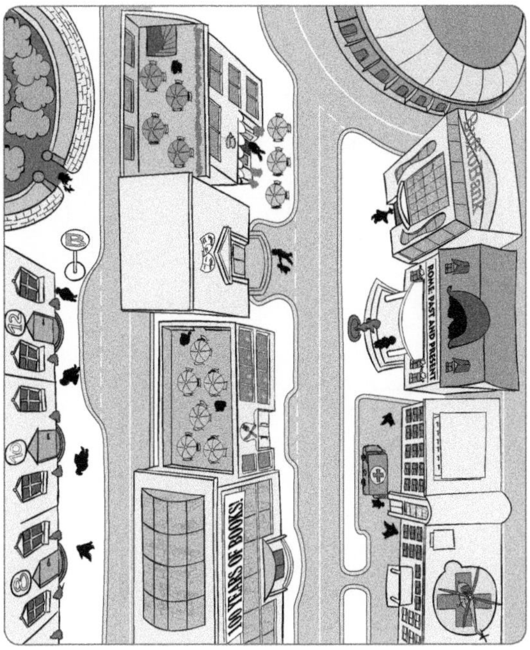

I live at 12 Albion Way. There's a small [0] *park* in my street. The bus stop is [1] ________ my house. The new football [2] ________ is in Alexander Avenue. The history [3] ________ is in Alexander Avenue too. It's [4] ________ the bank and the [5] ________. My mum's a doctor there. The Royal Theatre is a famous building. It's [6] ________ the bank. My friends and I don't go there often. We love eating ice cream at our favourite [7] ________ next to the theatre. And my parents love having dinner at the [8] ________ next to the theatre. The coolest building in the city is the [9] ________. It's got thousands of great books. My best friend's house is in my street, [10] ________ the library.

☐ / 10

name ______________________ class ______

5.4 Places in town (2) **B**

2 Match beginnings 1–5 with endings a–e.

0 I play volleyball at the sports [*f*]
1 I meet my friends at the swimming ☐
2 My friends and I go to the shopping ☐
3 The police ☐
4 There are a lot of people at the train ☐
5 There's a post ☐

a station. They're waiting for their train.
b office opposite the bank.
c station is in Haig Street.
d pool every weekend.
e centre on Saturdays and we hang out together.
f centre after school.

☐ / 5

name ______________________ class ______

5.6 Adjectives **B**

3 Look at the adjectives in bold. Use adjectives with the opposite meaning.

0 The forest isn't a **safe** place. There are a lot of *d a n g e r o u s* animals there.
1 My dad doesn't like _ _ _ _ _ _ houses. He likes **old** houses.
2 On Saturday morning the streets are **busy** but they are _ _ _ _ _ on Sunday morning.
3 The History Museum is **boring** but the Science Museum is _ _ _ _ _ _ _ _ _ _ _ _.
4 The living room is _ _ _ _ _ but my bedroom is **clean**.
5 We don't live in a **big** city. We live in a _ _ _ _ _ town.

☐ / 5

Your total score ☐ / 20

© Pearson Education Limited 2017 PHOTOCOPIABLE

6 Vocabulary Check A

name ______________________ class ______

6.1 Jobs

A

1 Look at the pictures and write the jobs.

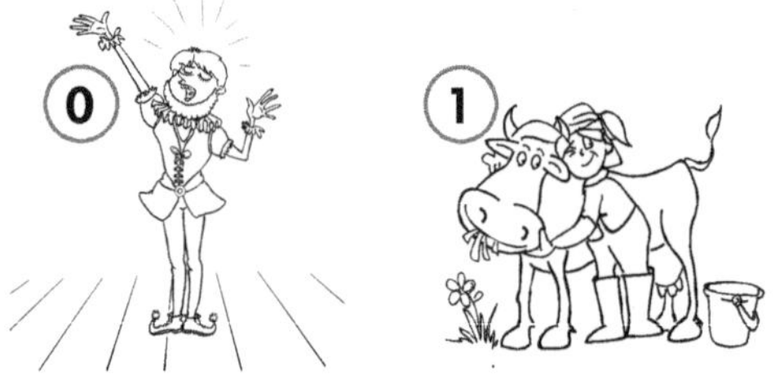

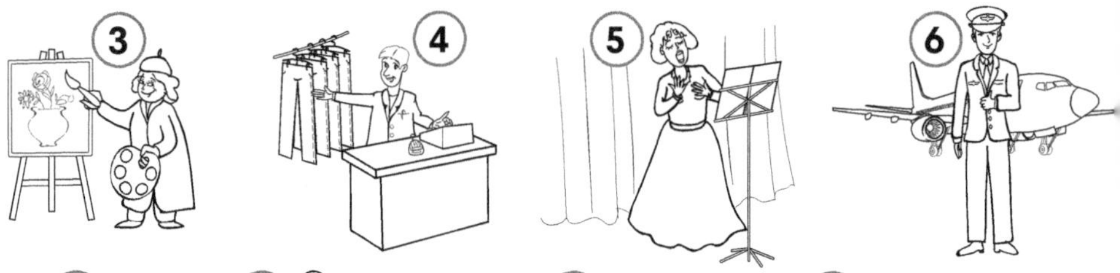

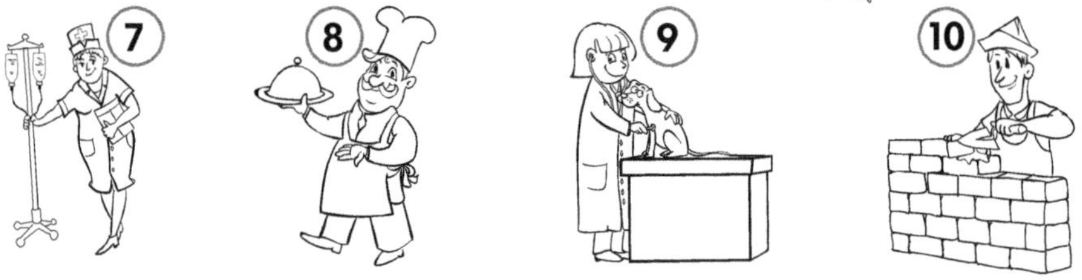

0 a c t o r

1 f _ _ _ _ _

2 p _ _ _ _ _ o _ _ _ _ _ _

3 a _ _ _ _ _

4 s _ _ _ a _ _ _ _ _ _ _ _ _

5 s _ _ _ _ _

6 p _ _ _ _

7 n _ _ _ _

8 c _ _ _

9 v _ _

10 b _ _ _ _ _ _

☐ / [10]

2 What's their job? Complete the dialogues.

0 **A:** A lot of people watch me when I work. I usually work in the evening.
B: I know! You're an **a** c t o r!

1 **A:** I work with a ball, I run a lot and I work with ten other people in a team.
B: That's easy! You're a **f** _ _ _ _ _ _ _ _ _ _.

2 **A:** I work in a hospital and I help ill people.
B: I think you're a **d** _ _ _ _ _.

3 **A:** I drive all day and people need me to go to work or to school.
B: You're a **b** _ _ **d** _ _ _ _ _.

4 **A:** I love my job because I work with children in a school.
B: You're a **t** _ _ _ _ _ _, of course!

5 **A:** I work inside a building and I use a computer in an office.
B: I'm sure you're an **o** _ _ _ _ _ **w** _ _ _ _ _.

☐ / [5]

---

name ______________________ class ______

6.5 Jobs at home

A

3 Circle the correct word.

Every Saturday morning, my brother Alan and I [0]*tidy* / *wash* our bedrooms and [1]*do* / *make* our beds. Mum and Dad [2]*do* / *have* the shopping at the supermarket. Then Alan [3]*washes* / *watches* Mum's car – it's always dirty! Dad and I work in the garden. In the afternoon, Mum and Dad visit their friends and Alan and I [4]*take after* / *look after* our little sister. I always [5]*send* / *empty* the bin at night – it's usually full!

☐ / [5]

Your total score ☐ / [20]

6 Vocabulary Check B

name ______________________ class ______

6.1 Jobs

B

1 Look at the pictures and write the jobs.

0 a *ctor*

1 s _ _ _ _ _

2 s _ _ _ a _ _ _ _ _ _ _ _ _

3 n _ _ _ _

4 b _ _ _ _ _ _

5 v _ _

6 p _ _ _ _ _ o _ _ _ _ _ _

7 f _ _ _ _ _

8 c _ _ _

9 a _ _ _ _ _

10 p _ _ _ _

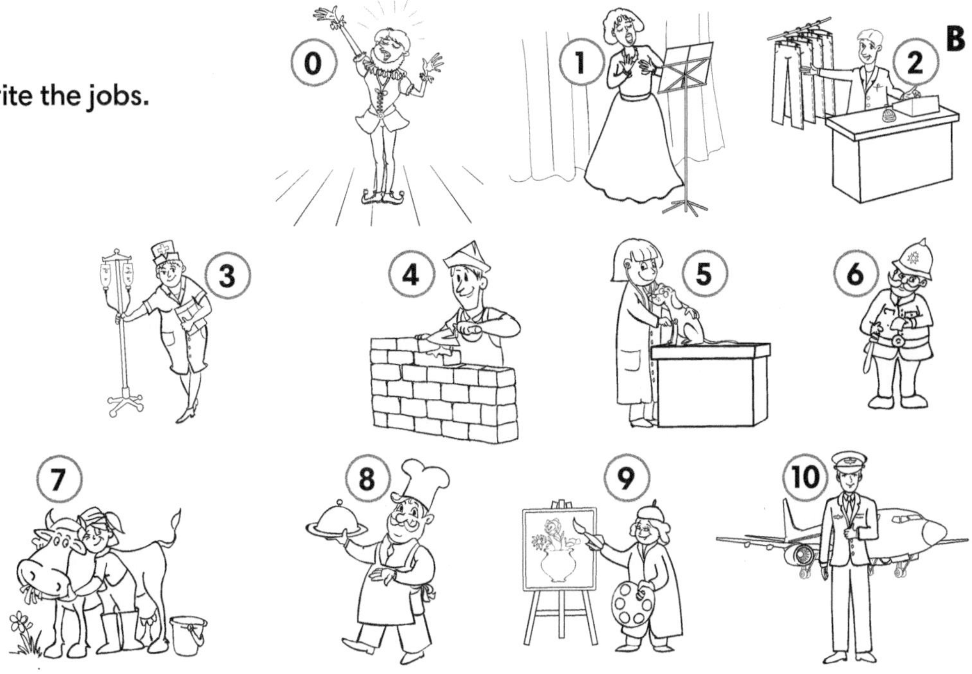

☐ / 10

2 What's their job? Complete the dialogues.

0 **A:** A lot of people watch me when I work. I usually work in the evening.
B: I know! You're an **a** *ctor*!

1 **A:** I drive all day and people need me to go to work or to school.
B: I think you're a **b** _ _ **d** _ _ _ _ _.

2 **A:** I work in an office and I use a computer a lot.
B: You're an **o** _ _ _ _ _ **w** _ _ _ _ _.

3 **A:** I work with young people in a school and I love my job.
B: That's easy! You're a **t** _ _ _ _ _ _!

4 **A:** I work in a hospital and I help ill people.
B: I think you're a **d** _ _ _ _ _.

5 **A:** I run a lot and I work with a ball. There are eleven people in my team.
B: That's easy! You're a **f** _ _ _ _ _ _ _ _ _.

☐ / 5

---

name ______________________ class ______

6.5 Jobs at home

B

3 Circle the correct word.

Every Saturday morning, my sister Beth and I [0]*tidy* / *wash* our bedrooms and [1]*make* / do our beds. Then I [2]*take* / *walk* the dog. After lunch Beth [3]*watches* / *washes* the dishes. In the evening, Mum and Dad sometimes go to the cinema and Beth and I [4]*look after* / *take after* our baby brother. Dad [5]*sends* / *empties* the bin at night – it's usually full!

☐ / 5

Your total score ☐ / 20

7 Vocabulary Check A

name ______________________ class ______

7.1 Transport nouns and verbs A

1 Use the pictures and the words in the box to complete the sentences.

arrived	got off	left	took	~~travelled~~

0 Dad *travelled* to London yesterday. He went there by 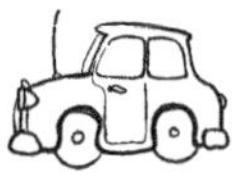 *car*.

1 I got on the 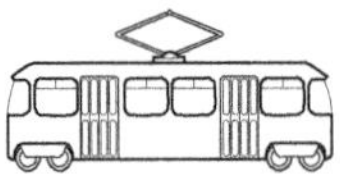 ____________ at five past nine and ____________ at thirteen minutes past ten.

2 Anna went to the island by 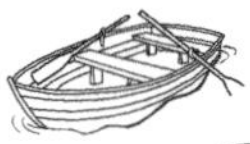 ____________. She ____________ the house early this morning.

3 They went to Paris by 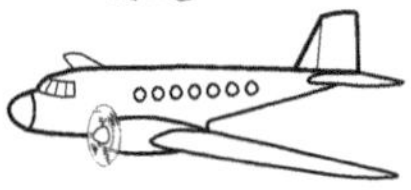 ____________. They ____________ there at eleven o'clock.

4 Uncle Stan loves riding his 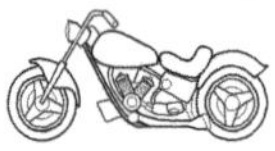 ____________. It's fast and exciting.

5 I go to school on 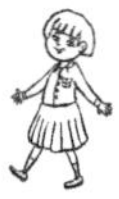 ____________. I like walking.

6 Howard ____________ the number 59 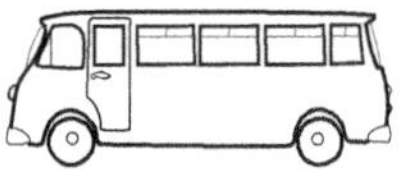 ____________ to work this morning.

☐ / 10

name ______________________ class ______

7.2 Travel equipment A

2 Match sentences 1–5 with travel equipment a–e.

0 You take photos with it. [f]
1 You wear these on your face when it is sunny. ☐
2 You put your things in it and you carry it on your back. ☐
3 Your read about places in it. ☐
4 You use this to see when it is dark. ☐
5 You sleep in it when you go camping. ☐

a backpack
b torch
c sunglasses
d guidebook
e tent
f camera

☐ / 5

name ______________________ class ______

7.3 Things to do on holiday A

3 Complete the sentences.

When we go on holiday …

0 My brother and I like visiting **m** *u s e u m* **s** but Dad doesn't like looking at old things.
1 My mum loves going **s** _ _ _ _ _ _ _ _ _ **g** but my dad thinks old buildings are boring. And he hates walking around cities!
2 We don't stay in expensive **h** _ _ _ _ **s**. We always go camping.
3 I often buy **s** _ _ _ _ _ _ _ **s** from interesting shops, like postcards and toy animals.
4 My sister takes **p** _ _ _ _ **s** of the beautiful places we visit.
5 My sister and I meet a lot of interesting people and we often make **f** _ _ _ _ _ **s** with them.

☐ / 5

Your total score ☐ / 20

7 Vocabulary Check B

name ______________________ class ______

7.1 Transport nouns and verbs **B**

1 Use the pictures and the words in the box to complete the sentences.

arrived got off left took ~~travelled~~

0 Dad _travelled_ to London yesterday. He went there by 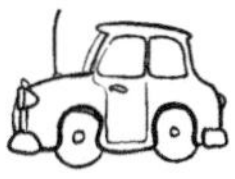 _car_.

1 Annette likes walking. She goes to school on 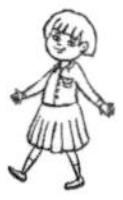 __________.

2 Muriel and Keith went to Madrid by 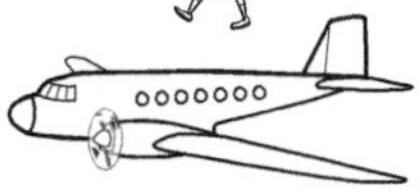 __________. They __________ there at two o'clock yesterday afternoon.

3 I __________ the number 16 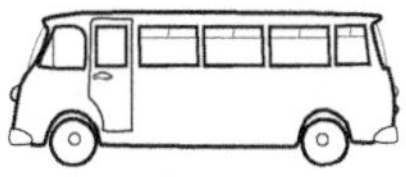 __________ to school this morning.

4 Aunt Beverly loves riding her new 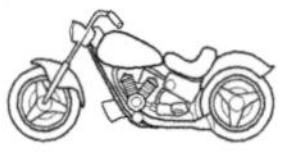 __________. It's very exciting.

5 Matthew got on the 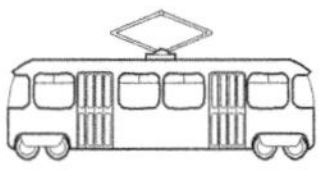 __________ at ten to eight and __________ at five minutes past nine.

6 Andrew went to the island by 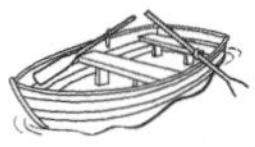 __________. He __________ the house yesterday morning.

[ ] / [10]

---

name ______________________ class ______

7.2 Travel equipment **B**

2 Match sentences 1–5 with travel equipment a–e.

0 You take photos with it. [_f_]
1 You put your things in it when you go on holiday. [ ]
2 Your read about places in it. [ ]
3 You sleep in it when you go camping. [ ]
4 You wear these on your face when it is sunny. [ ]
5 You use this to see when it is dark. [ ]

a suitcase
b sleeping bag
c sunglasses
d guidebook
e torch
f camera

[ ] / [5]

---

name ______________________ class ______

7.3 Things to do on holiday **B**

3 Complete the sentences.

When we go on holiday …

0 My brother and I like visiting **m** _u s e u m_ **s** but Dad doesn't like looking at old things.
1 My family and I sometimes have dinner at a **r** _ _ _ _ _ _ _ _ **t**. We love eating food from other countries.
2 Dad doesn't like going **s** _ _ _ _ _ _ _ _ _ **g** but Mum loves looking at old buildings.
3 We meet a lot of interesting people and we like making **f** _ _ _ _ _ **s**.
4 My brother often buys **s** _ _ _ _ _ _ _ **s** when he is on holiday. He's got a lot of toy animals from different countries in his bedroom.
5 My family and I usually stay in a cheap **h** _ _ _ **l**. We don't like camping.

[ ] / [5]

Your total score [ ] / [20]

name ______________________ class ______

8.1 Events

A

1 Complete the sentences with the words in the box.

barbecue birthday party concert fancy dress ~~film~~ match picnic play show sleepover talent competition

0 They're at the cinema and they're watching a *film*.
1 Mum and Dad made sandwiches for our ______________ on the beach.
2 I went to a ______________ on Saturday. My favourite musician played the piano.
3 My friends came to my house for a ______________. We had fun all night.
4 Kylie and her dad are at the stadium. They're watching a football ______________.
5 We're having a ______________ in the garden. Dad is cooking sausages.
6 I wore a beautiful costume to the ______________ party.
7 Joyce is thirteen years old today. There are a lot of people at her ______________.
8 I took part in a ______________ on TV. I didn't win but I was third.
9 The actors in the ______________ at the theatre were fantastic.
10 Who are the best dancers in the dance ______________?

[ ] / [10]

name ______________________ class ______

8.1 Ordinal numbers

A

2 Write the dates.

0	1	2	3	4	5
3rd May	15th August	26th December	11th November	30th October	9th June
the third of May	______	______	______	______	______
Mum's birthday!	Holiday for everyone!	I love the day after Christmas!	Maths test today	Piano lesson this afternoon	Buy flowers for Granny

[ ] / [5]

name ______________________ class ______

8.3 Types of music

A

3 Complete the sentences with the kinds of music.

0 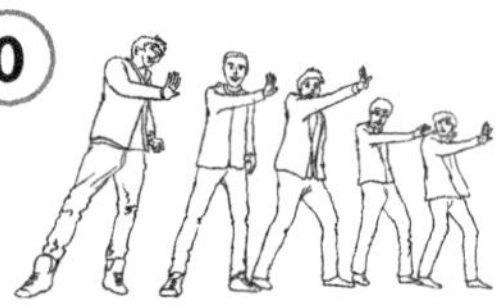
1 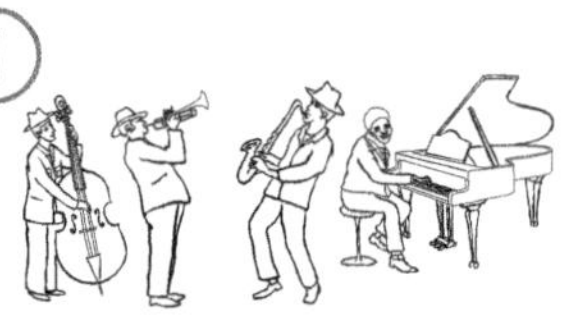
2 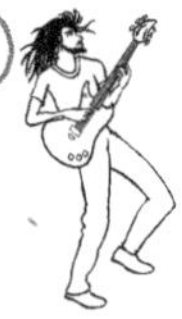
3 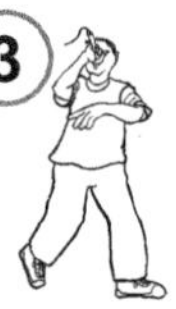
4 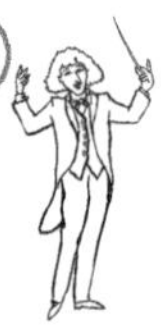
5 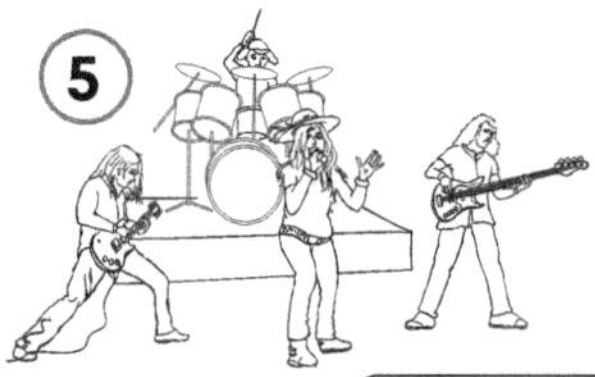

What kind of music do they like?
0 Amy likes p *o p*.
1 Jamie loves j _ _ _.
2 Jemima thinks r _ _ _ _ _ is the best kind of music.
3 Martine always listens to r _ _.
4 Hugo thinks c _ _ _ _ _ _ _ _ music is fantastic.
5 Lynne's favourite music is r _ _ _.

[ ] / [5]

Your total score [ ] / [20]

8 Vocabulary Check B

name ______________________ class ____

8.1 Events B

1 Complete the sentences with the words in the box.

barbecue birthday party concert fancy dress ~~film~~ match picnic play show sleepover talent competition

0 They're at the cinema and they're watching a *film*.
1 Hannah's friends went to her house for a ______________. They had fun all night.
2 Ben and I went to a ______________ last night and listened to our favourite band.
3 I enjoyed the ______________ at the theatre. The actors were fantastic.
4 Our neighbours are having a ______________ in the garden. Mr Bigg is cooking sausages for everyone.
5 Dora is twelve years old today. There are a lot of people at her ______________.
6 The best dancers in the dance ______________ are Tom and Mandy.
7 My sister took part in a ______________ on TV. People loved her!
8 We took sandwiches with us and had a ______________ in the park.
9 Chris and his dad are at the stadium. They're watching a football ______________.
10 Ewa wore a beautiful costume to the ______________ party.

☐ / 10

name ______________________ class ____

8.1 Ordinal numbers B

2 Write the dates.

0	1	2	3	4	5
3rd May	19th February	24th April	31st July	8th September	15th November
the third of May	______	______	______	______	______
Mum's birthday!	Snow all day …	Spring is here!	Holidays!	Geography test	Basketball practice today

☐ / 5

name ______________________ class ____

8.3 Types of music B

3 Complete the sentences with the kinds of music.

0
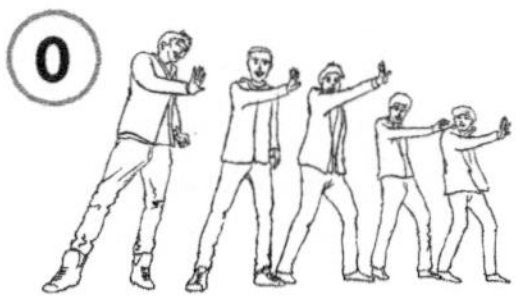
1
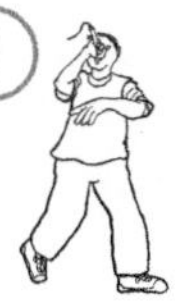
2
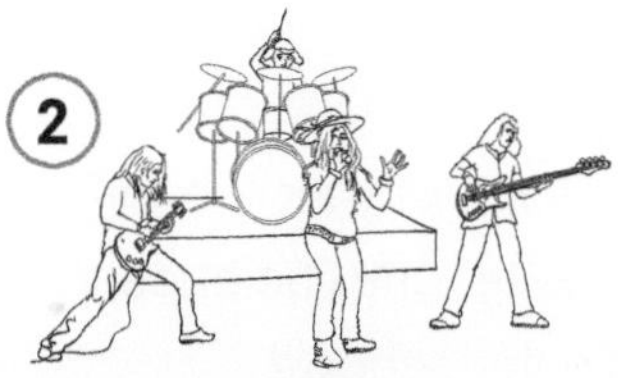
3
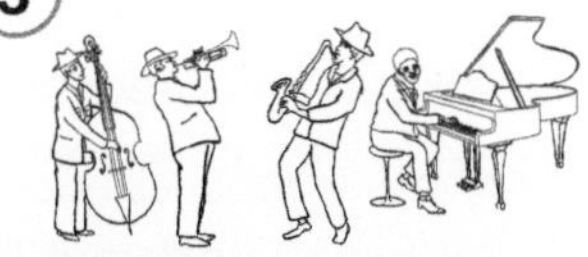
4
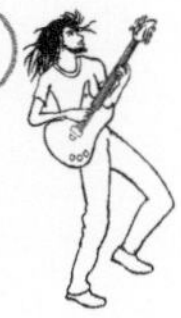
5
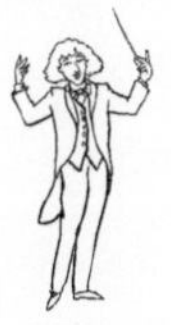

What kind of music do they like?
0 Amy likes **p** *o p*.
1 Max likes listening to **r** _ _.
2 Fay's favourite music is **r** _ _ _.
3 Joe usually listens to **j** _ _ _.
4 Henry thinks **r** _ _ _ _ _ is cool.
5 Eileen listens to **c** _ _ _ _ _ _ _ _ music on her mp3 player.

☐ / 5

Your total score ☐ / 20

© Pearson Education Limited 2017 PHOTOCOPIABLE

1 Grammar Check A

name _______________ class _______

1.2 Present Simple affirmative A

1 Use the correct form of the verbs.

0 Jake *walks* (walk) to school every morning.
1 Gerald ________ (wash) his hair every day.
2 Julia ________ (go) to bed late on Friday night.
3 Luke ________ (study) English at school.
4 I ________ (like) singing in the shower.
5 Rob ________ (walk) with his dog in the park.

[ ] / [5]

1.2 Adverbs of frequency

2 Put the words in the correct order.

0 often / I / homework / Jan / help / with / her
I often help Jan with her homework.
1 late / you / school / often / for / are
____
2 we / swimming / August / never / go / after
____
3 with / sometimes / football / my dad / I / play
____
4 school / always / my bike / to / ride / I
____
5 Jess / goes / to / on Friday / the cinema / usually
____

[ ] / [5]

name _______________ class _______

1.3 Present Simple negative, questions and short answers A

3 Complete the dialogue with the words in the box. There is one extra word.

~~do~~ doesn't doesn't don't no we yes

A: [0]*Do* you walk to school every day?
B: [1]________, I do.
A: Does Mrs Gregson teach Maths at your school?
B: No, she [2]________. She teaches Science.
A: Do you and your friends enjoy school?
B: Yes, [3]________ do but my big sister [4]________ like it.
A: Why?
B: I [5]________ know.

[ ] / [5]

Your total score [ ] / [15]

1 Grammar Check B

name _______________ class _______

1.2 Present Simple affirmative B

1 Use the correct form of the verbs.

0 Jake *walks* (walk) to school every morning.
1 Beth ________ (brush) her teeth after breakfast.
2 Tessa ________ (cook) lunch for the family.
3 Jim and I ________ (do) our homework at home.
4 Roy ________ (love) listening to music.
5 Paula ________ (study) English in her room.

[ ] / [5]

1.2 Adverbs of frequency

2 Put the words in the correct order.

0 often / I / homework / Jan / help / with / her
I often help Jan with her homework.
1 we / for a walk / take / Paul's dog / sometimes
____
2 my aunt / at the weekend / us / usually / visits
____
3 for / never / am / school / late / I
____
4 goes / in summer / Tim / always / swimming
____
5 with / hang out / my friends / I / often / on Friday
____

[ ] / [5]

name _______________ class _______

1.3 Present Simple negative, questions and short answers B

3 Complete the dialogue with the words in the box. There is one extra word.

~~do~~ does doesn't don't no we yes

A: [0]*Do* you walk to school every day?
B: [1]________, I don't. I ride my bike.
A: Do you and your brother enjoy school?
B: Yes, [2]________ do but my sister [3]________ like it.
A: Why?
B: I [4]________ know. Ask her!
A: [5]________ Mr Wilkinson teach you English?
B: Yes, and he's a great teacher!

[ ] / [5]

Your total score [ ] / [15]

2 Grammar Check A

name ______ class ______

2.2 Countable and uncountable nouns, *some/any* A

1 Circle the correct answer.

Pete: What's in the fridge, Annie?
Annie: Well, I can see [0]___ apples, [1]___ butter, [2]___ egg, [3]___ lemons, [4]___ milk and [5]___ vegetables.
Pete: Let's go to the supermarket! We need some food!

0 a an (b two)　　3 a a　b three
1 a a　b some　　4 a a　b some
2 a a　b an　　5 a a　b some

☐ / 5

2 Complete the sentences and questions with *a/an*, *some* or *any*.

0 There isn't _an_ orange in the kitchen.
1 Are there _____ tomatoes? Let's make a pizza.
2 There are _____ biscuits in the cupboard.
3 Is there _____ sausage for me? I'm hungry.
4 There isn't _____ flour in the kitchen.
5 There aren't _____ potatoes. Sorry, no chips!

☐ / 5

name ______ class ______

2.3 *How much ...?/How many ...? a lot of* A

3 Circle the correct answer.

0 **A:** (*How much*) / *How many* water is there?
B: There's a lot of water.

1 **A:** *How much / How many* sugar is there?
B: There's a lot of sugar.

2 **A:** *How much / How many* apples are there?
B: There are twelve apples.

3 **A:** How much chocolate is there?
B: *There's / There are* four bars of chocolate.

4 **A:** *How much / How many* jars of jam are there?
B: There are two jars.

5 **A:** How much juice is there?
B: There's *two / a lot of* juice.

☐ / 5

Your total score ☐ / 15

2 Grammar Check B

name ______ class ______

2.2 Countable and uncountable nouns, *some/any* B

1 Circle the correct answer.

Pete: What's in the fridge, Annie?
Annie: Well, I can see [0]___ apples, [1]___ lemons, [2]___ egg, [3]___ butter, [4]___ vegetables and [5]___ milk.
Pete: Let's go to the supermarket! We need some food!

0 a an (b two)　　3 a a　b some
1 a a　b four　　4 a a　b some
2 a an　b some　　5 a a　b some

☐ / 5

2 Complete the sentences and questions with *a/an*, *some* or *any*.

0 There isn't _an_ orange in the kitchen.
1 Are there _____ sausages for me? I'm hungry.
2 There aren't _____ potatoes. Sorry, no chips!
3 Is there _____ chocolate?
4 There's _____ flour in the cupboard.
5 There's _____ cupcake on the table.

☐ / 5

name ______ class ______

2.3 *How much ...?/How many ...? a lot of* B

3 Circle the correct answer.

0 **A:** (*How much*) / *How many* water is there?
B: There's a lot of water.

1 **A:** *How much / How many* cans of cola are there?
B: There are five cans.

2 **A:** *How much / How many* sugar is there?
B: There's a lot of sugar.

3 **A:** *How much / How many* apples are there?
B: There are a lot of apples.

4 **A:** How much water is there?
B: There's *three / a lot of* water.

5 **A:** How much chocolate is there?
B: *There's / There are* a bar of chocolate.

☐ / 5

Your total score ☐ / 15

© Pearson Education Limited 2017 PHOTOCOPIABLE

3 Grammar Check A

name ______________________ class ______

3.2 Present Continuous affirmative and negative A

1 Complete the sentences with the correct form of the Present Continuous.

0 The children *are watching* (watch) TV now.
1 Suzie ____________ (study) in her bedroom.
2 You ____________ (talk) to your aunt on the phone.
3 My friend and I ____________ (chat) online.
4 Dan and Carla ____________ (write) emails to their grandparents.
5 I ____________ (have) a shower! I can't talk now.

[ ] / [5]

2 Use the short form of the Present Continuous.

0 My brother and I *aren't playing* computer games. (not play)
1 I ____________ to music with my new headphones. (not listen)
2 The teacher ____________ the Internet. (surf)
3 They ____________ to school. (run)
4 You ____________ at the party. (not dance)
5 Ivy ____________ her homework. (not do)

[ ] / [5]

name ______________________ class ______

3.3 Present Continuous questions and short answers A

3 Use the words in the box in the dialogues.

am ~~are~~ aren't is isn't we

Maria: Hi, Angela. It's me, Maria.
Angela: Hi, Maria.
Maria: [0]*Are* you enjoying the party?
Angela: Yes, I [1]________.
Maria: Are you and your friends dancing?
Angela: Yes, [2]________ are.
Maria: [3]________ your granny sitting in the garden?
Angela: No, she [4]________. She's dancing too!
Maria: Are your parents dancing?
Angela: No, they [5]________. They're talking to my friends' parents!

[ ] / [5]

Your total score [ ] / [15]

3 Grammar Check B

nname ______________________ class ______

3.2 Present Continuous affirmative and negative B

1 Complete the sentences with the correct form of the Present Continuous.

0 The children *are watching* (watch) TV now.
1 I ____________ (have) lunch! I can't talk now.
2 Marcus ____________ (chat) to his friend online.
3 My sister and I ____________ (study) in our bedroom.
4 Frances and Joe ____________ (make) pizzas.
5 You ____________ (play) football in the garden.

[ ] / [5]

2 Use the short form of the Present Continuous.

0 My brother and I *aren't playing* computer games. (not play)
1 The teacher ____________ in the staff room. (sit)
2 You ____________ the party. (not enjoy)
3 I ____________ TV now. (not watch)
4 They ____________ to school. (run)
5 Karen ____________ karate now. (not do)

[ ] / [5]

name ______________________ class ______

3.3 Present Continuous questions and short answers B

3 Use the words in the box in the dialogues.

'm ~~are~~ are is isn't they

George: Hi, Alec. It's me, George.
Alec: Hi, George.
George: [0]*Are* you enjoying the party?
Alec: Yes, we [1]________.
George: Are you dancing?
Alec: No, I [2]________ not.
George: [3]________ your grandad dancing?
Alec: No, he [4]________. He's eating ice cream.
George: Are your friends' parents dancing?
Alec: No, [5]________ aren't.

[ ] / [5]

Your total score [ ] / [15]

4 Grammar Check A

name ______ class ______

4.2 Comparative adjectives A

1 Complete the sentences with the comparative form of the adjectives.

0 The Nile is *longer* (long) than the Colorado.
1 Warm weather is __________ (nice) than cold weather!
2 Spain is __________ (hot) than Poland.
3 Are dogs __________ (good) pets than cats?
4 Are tigers __________ (dangerous) than lions?
5 Alan is __________ (friendly) than Bob.

[ ] / [5]

name ______ class ______

4.3 Superlative adjectives A

2 Complete the sentences with the superlative form of the adjectives.

0 *cute animals:* rabbits* / hamsters** / puppies***
Puppies are the cutest animals in the group.
1 *high mountains:* Mount Everest*** / Mont Blanc* / Mount Kilimanjaro**
____
2 *intelligent animals:* cats** / dogs*** / rats*
____
3 *easy languages:* English*** / French* / Polish**
____
4 *big cities:* Zurich* / Paris** / Tokyo***
____
5 *exciting sports:* football*** / hockey* / tennis**
____

[ ] / [5]

3 Circle the correct answer.

0 That is *worse* / *(the worst)* place in the world!
1 I think Madrid is *more beautiful* / *the most beautiful* than Birmingham.
2 Who is *better* / *the best* student in your class?
3 The baby's chair is *lower* / *the lowest* chair in the house.
4 Who is *hungrier* / *the hungriest*: you or your dad?
5 Is Poland *bigger* / *the biggest* country in Europe?

[ ] / [5]

Your total score [ ] / [15]

4 Grammar Check B

name ______ class ______

4.2 Comparative adjectives B

1 Complete the sentences with the comparative form of the adjectives.

0 The Nile is *longer* (long) than the Colorado.
1 Italy is __________ (hot) than the UK.
2 Are lions __________ (dangerous) than tigers?
3 Warm weather is __________ (nice) than cold weather!
4 Gregory is __________ (friendly) than Wanda.
5 Rats are __________ (bad) pets than snakes.

[ ] / [5]

name ______ class ______

4.3 Superlative adjectives B

2 Complete the sentences with the superlative form of the adjectives.

0 *cute animals:* rabbits* / hamsters** / puppies***
Puppies are the cutest animals in the group.
1 *easy languages:* French* / Spanish** / English***
____
2 *exciting sports:* sailing* / skiing*** / tennis**
____
3 *big cities:* London*** / Manchester** / Glasgow*
____
4 *intelligent animals:* rats* / cats** / dogs***
____
5 *high mountains:* Mont Blanc* / Mount Everest*** / Mount Kenya**
____

[ ] / [5]

3 Circle the correct answer.

0 That is *worse* / *(the worst)* place in the world!
1 My phone is *newer* / *the newest* phone in the class.
2 Is Germany *bigger* / *the biggest* country in Europe?
3 I think Rome is *more beautiful* / *the most beautiful* than London.
4 Who is *better* / *the best* student in your class?
5 Who is *hungrier* / *the hungriest*: Harry or Bertie?

[ ] / [5]

Your total score [ ] / [15]

5 Grammar Check A

name class

5.2 Past Simple *to be* affirmative and negative A

1 Circle the correct word.

Hi Andrew,
My family and I [0]*wasn't* / *weren't* at home yesterday evening. Mum and Dad [1]*was* / *were* at the cinema and I [2]*was* / *were* at the park with my friends. [3]*There was* / *There were* a concert but [4]*there wasn't* / *there weren't* a lot of people because it [5]*was* / *were* very cold.
What's your news?
Maureen

☐ / 5

name class

5.3 Past Simple *to be* questions and short answers A

2 Put the words in the correct order.

0 exciting / was / holiday / your / ?
Was your holiday exciting?
1 your family / was / home / at / yesterday / ?
____
2 any / were / in / there / the garden / apples / ?
____
3 Kevin / was / night / last / where / ?
____
4 yesterday / at / there / a party / was / school / ?
____
5 at / was / night / the theatre / last / Maria / ?
____

☐ / 5

3 Use short answers: positive [✓] or negative [✗].

0 A: Were the students in the park last night?
B: *Yes, they were.* [✓] / *No, they weren't.* [✗]
1 A: Were the trains late again yesterday?
B: __________ [✗]
2 A: Was the cat in the garden last week?
B: __________ [✓]
3 A: Was there a good film on TV yesterday?
B: __________ [✓]
4 A: Was the restaurant busy last Saturday?
B: __________ [✗]
5 A: Were there any jeans in the shop last week?
B: __________ [✗]

☐ / 5

Your total score ☐ / 15

5 Grammar Check B

name class

5.2 Past Simple *to be* affirmative and negative B

1 Circle the correct word.

Hi Maisie,
Rob, David and I [0]*wasn't* / *weren't* at home yesterday evening. I [1]*was* / *were* at the park with my friends. [2]*There wasn't* / *There weren't* a concert but [3]*there was* / *there were* a lot of people because it [4]*was* / *were* a warm evening. Rob and David [5]*was* / *were* at the football stadium.
What's your news?
Jules

☐ / 5

name class

5.3 Past Simple *to be* questions and short answers B

2 Put the words in the correct order.

0 your / exciting / was / holiday / ?
Was your holiday exciting?
1 Peter / last / was / where / night / ?
____
2 the restaurant / at / was / week / last / Diana / ?
____
3 was / your family / last / home / night / at / ?
____
4 in / was / there / a party / the street / yesterday / ?
____
5 the garden / any / were / in / there / flowers / ?
____

☐ / 5

3 Use short answers: positive [✓] or negative [✗].

0 A: Were the students in the park last night?
B: *Yes, they were.* [✓] / *No, they weren't.* [✗]
1 A: Was there a cake on the table this morning?
B: __________ [✗]
2 A: Were there any dogs in the park yesterday?
B: __________ [✓]
3 A: Was the film last Sunday interesting?
B: __________ [✗]
4 A: Was our cat in the garden last night?
B: __________ [✓]
5 A: Last summer, were the beaches clean?
B: __________ [✗]

☐ / 5

Your total score ☐ / 15

6 Grammar Check A

name ______________________ class ______

6.2 Past Simple affirmative regular verbs A

1 Complete the text with the Past Simple form of the verbs in the box. There is one extra verb.

~~arrive~~ cook play stay stop try watch

Yesterday I [0] *arrived* home from work at six o'clock. Then I [1] ________ with my dog, Rex, in the garden. It was cold so after half an hour, we [2] ________ our game and I [3] ________ TV. Rex [4] ________ with me. He loves watching TV! At seven o'clock I was hungry so I [5] ________ to make some pancakes. They were delicious!

☐ / [5]

name ______________________ class ______

6.3 Past Simple affirmative irregular verbs A

2 Use the Past Simple form of the verbs in bold.

0 I **am** happy but yesterday I *was* very sad.
1 Larry sometimes **goes** to school by bus but last week he ________ by train.
2 Brenda usually **meets** her friends at school but yesterday she ________ them in the park.
3 Mum often **makes** pizza for lunch but yesterday she ________ chicken and vegetables.
4 Uncle Alfie often **comes** to our house for dinner but last Saturday he ________ for lunch.
5 I usually **have** a shower before breakfast but yesterday I ________ a shower after breakfast.

☐ / [5]

3 Complete the sentences with the Past Simple form of the verbs in the box. There is one extra verb.

~~be~~ drink eat feel have meet take

0 The weather *was* cold and rainy last weekend.
1 Sheila ______ a glass of orange juice yesterday.
2 The children ________ all the apples yesterday!
3 Angela and Martin ________ a lot of photos yesterday. Photography is their hobby.
4 We ______ our friends in the park last Monday.
5 Mum worked all day and she ________ tired.

☐ / [5]

Your total score ☐ / [15]

6 Grammar Check B

nname ______________________ class ______

6.2 Past Simple affirmative regular verbs B

1 Complete the text with the Past Simple form of the verbs in the box. There is one extra verb.

~~arrive~~ cook play stop tidy try walk

Yesterday I [0] *arrived* home from work at six o'clock. I was hungry so I [1] ________ to make some pancakes. They were terrible so I [2] ________ to a restaurant in the town centre for dinner. Then I [3] ________ computer games for an hour. At eleven o'clock I was bored so [4] ________ playing and I [5] ________ the living room.

☐ / [5]

name ______________________ class ______

6.3 Past Simple affirmative irregular verbs B

2 Use the Past Simple form of the verbs in bold.

0 I **am** happy but yesterday I *was* very sad.
1 Dad often **makes** sandwiches for lunch but yesterday he ________ chicken and potatoes.
2 I usually **have** breakfast at seven o'clock but yesterday I ________ breakfast at ten to eight.
3 Aunt Mabel often **comes** to our house for lunch but last Sunday she ________ for dinner.
4 Mimi sometimes **goes** to school by car but last week she ________ on foot.
5 Stan usually **meets** his friends at the Café Italia but yesterday he ________ them at home.

☐ / [5]

3 Complete the sentences with the Past Simple form of the verbs in the box. There is one extra verb.

~~be~~ drink eat have feel meet take

0 The weather *was* cold and rainy last weekend.
1 The children ________ a Music lesson yesterday.
2 Timothy and Sally ________ some photos yesterday. Photography is their hobby.
3 We ________ our friends in the park last Friday.
4 Claudette ______ ill so she went to the doctor.
5 Dan ________ a glass of milk this morning.

☐ / [5]

Your total score ☐ / [15]

© Pearson Education Limited 2017 PHOTOCOPIABLE

7 Grammar Check A

name ______ class ______

7.2 Past Simple negative A

1 Use the negative Past Simple form of the verbs in the box.

~~arrive~~ do eat make stop study

0 Mum *didn't arrive* home early. She was late.
1 It rained all day. It ______.
2 I ______ for school because I was ill.
3 We ______ karate yesterday.
4 The students ______ any posters at school.
5 The children ______ a lot of food.

[ ] / [5]

name ______ class ______

7.3 Past Simple questions and short answers A

2 Write questions. Use the words in bold.

0 I went to school by bus. (**Sam**?)
Did Sam go to school by bus?
1 Rick and I slept for ten hours last night. (**you**?)
______ for ten hours last night?
2 Mr Dug stayed in an expensive hotel. (**Mr Fey**?)
______ in an expensive hotel?
3 The children drank juice at the party. (**their mum**?)
______ juice at the party?
4 You and Oscar took a taxi to the station. (**they**?)
______ a taxi to the station?
5 I had a Music lesson yesterday. (**you**?)
______ a Music lesson yesterday?

[ ] / [5]

3 Use short answers: positive [✓] or negative [✗].

0 **A:** Did you watch TV last night?
B: *Yes, I did.* [✓] / **B:** *No, I didn't.* [✗]
1 **A:** Did your mum take the dog for a walk yesterday? **B:** ______ [✗]
2 **A:** Did Terry and Lily meet their friends at the shopping centre? **B:** ______ [✓]
3 **A:** Did I play the piano well? **B:** ______ [✗]
4 **A:** Did the plane leave at nine o'clock?
B: ______ [✓]
5 **A:** Did Harold ride his motorbike to work?
B: ______ [✗]

[ ] / [5]

Your total score [ ] / [15]

7 Grammar Check B

name ______ class ______

7.2 Past Simple negative B

1 Use the negative Past Simple form of the verbs in the box.

~~arrive~~ buy do drink stop text

0 Mum *didn't arrive* home early. She was late.
1 Emma ______ the dress. It was expensive.
2 Gerry and Mark ______ judo yesterday.
3 They studied all day. They ______.
4 We ______ the water from the river.
5 I ______ Jill. I phoned her.

[ ] / [5]

name ______ class ______

7.3 Past Simple questions and short answers B

2 Write questions. Use the words in bold.

0 I went to school by bus. (**Sam**?)
Did Sam go to school by bus?
1 The children ate cupcakes at the party. (**you**?)
______ cupcakes at the party?
2 We had a French lesson yesterday. (**Jenny**?)
______ a French lesson yesterday?
3 John watched the film yesterday. (**his mum**?)
______ the film yesterday?
4 The dog slept on the sofa last night. (**the cat**?)
______ on the sofa last night?
5 Mum took a taxi to the station. (**Dad**?)
______ a taxi to the station?

[ ] / [5]

3 Use short answers: positive [✓] or negative [✗].

0 **A:** Did you watch TV last night?
B: *Yes, I did.* [✓] / **B:** *No, I didn't.* [✗]
1 **A:** Did Billy look after his sister?
B: ______ [✗]
2 **A:** Did I sing the song well? **B:** ______ [✓]
3 **A:** Did the lesson start at nine o'clock?
B: ______ [✗]
4 **A:** Did Beth and Matt take the dogs for a walk yesterday? **B:** ______ [✓]
5 **A:** Did you and Yvette meet your friends in town?
B: ______ [✗]

[ ] / [5]

Your total score [ ] / [15]

8 Grammar Check A

name ______________________ class ________

8.2 *be going to* A

1 Use the correct form of *be going to*.

0 I *'m going to see* (see) a play tomorrow.
1 ______________ (you and Jack / buy) some food from the supermarket?
2 Our teacher ______________ (show) us a film about tigers this afternoon.
3 Sandy and I ______________ (not play) tennis at the weekend.
4 I ______________ (watch) TV at the weekend.
5 ______________ (your uncle / visit) you tonight?

[ ] / 5

2 Use the words in the box in the dialogues.

are ~~going~~ no study to we

A: Is Nick [0]*going* to look after his sister tonight?
B: Yes, he is.

A: Are you and I going to [1]________ tonight?
B: Yes, [2]________ are.

A: Are you going [3]________ download some songs?
B: [4]________, I'm not.

A: [5]________ Tim's friends going to come to the party?
B: Yes, they are.

[ ] / 5

name ______________________ class ________

8.3 Revision of questions A

3 Complete the questions.

0 Sue and Don are Olivia's best friends.
Are Sue and Don Olivia's best friends?
1 You can play the guitar.
______________ the guitar?
2 Jack has got a pet rabbit.
______________ a pet rabbit?
3 Morag does karate at the weekend.
______________ karate at the weekend?
4 The children are eating apples.
______________ apples?
5 We slept in a tent in the summer.
______________ in a tent in the summer?

[ ] / 5

Your total score [ ] / 15

8 Grammar Check B

name ______________________ class ________

8.2 *be going to* B

1 Use the correct form of *be going to*.

0 I *'m going to see* (see) a play tomorrow.
1 Lisa and Claude ______________ (not go) swimming this weekend.
2 ______________ (you / watch) TV?
3 Mr Stuart ______________ (not cook) dinner for his family tonight.
4 I ______________ (visit) my aunt tonight.
5 ______________ (you and I / meet) on Saturday?

[ ] / 5

2 Use the words in the box in the dialogues.

aren't blow ~~going~~ is to yes

A: Is Nick [0]*going* to look after his sister tonight?
B: Yes, he is.

A: Are all your friends going [1]________ come to the party?
B: [2]________, they are.

A: Are you and Keith going to [3]________ up balloons for the party?
B: No, we [4]________.

A: [5]________ Lacy going to do her homework?
B: No, she isn't.

[ ] / 5

name ______________________ class ________

8.3 Revision of questions B

3 Complete the questions.

0 Sue and Don are Olivia's best friends.
Are Sue and Don Olivia's best friends?
1 Piotr goes sailing at the weekend.
______________ sailing at the weekend?
2 We wore costumes to the party.
______________ costumes to the party?
3 Gemma can take great photos.
______________ great photos?
4 Granny and Grandad are sitting in the garden.
______________ in the garden?
5 The children have got new laptops.
______________ new laptops?

[ ] / 5

Your total score [ ] / 15

Get started! Language Test A

name ______________________ class ________

Vocabulary

1 Look at the pictures. Complete the sentences.

[0]

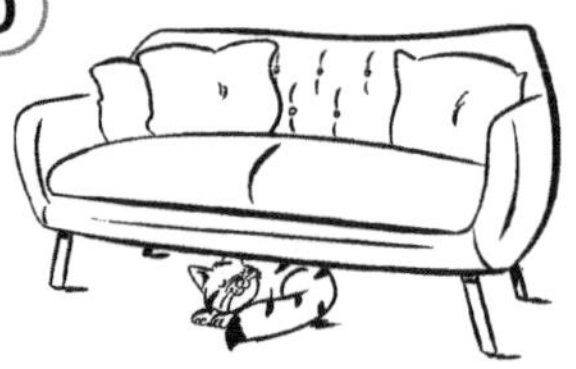

[1]

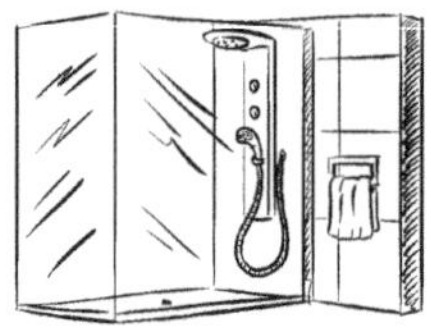

[2]

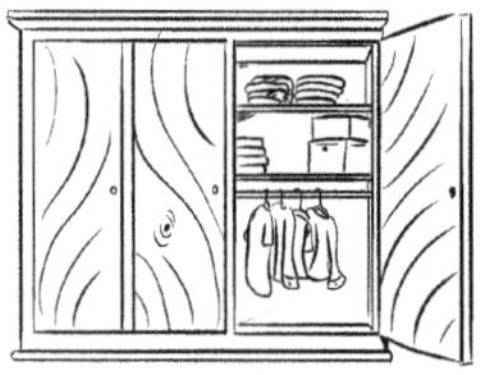

[3]

[4]

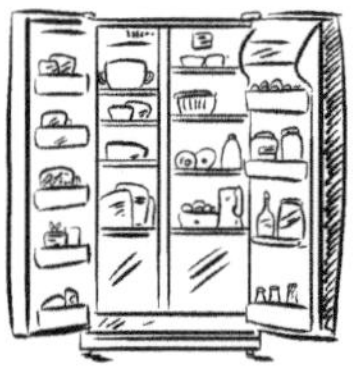

[5]

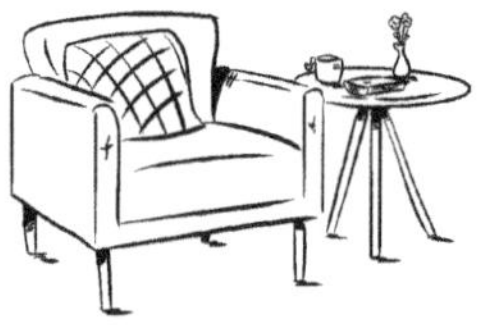

0 The cat is u*nder* the sofa.
1 The **s**__________ is in the bathroom.
2 The clothes are in the **w**__________.
3 The books are on the **s**__________.
4 The **f**__________ is in the kitchen.
5 The table is **n**__________ **t**__________ the armchair.

☐ / 5

2 Find the odd one out.

0	Tuesday	Thursday	(Birthday)	Sunday
1	Germany	Italy	Poland	American
2	Trainers	Hoodie	Jumper	T-shirt
3	Old	Clever	New	Big
4	Argentinian	Chinese	France	Turkish
5	Summer	February	April	September

☐ / 5

3 Match beginnings 1–5 with endings a–e.

0 Carl can play	[*f*]	**a**	Italian.
1 I can draw	☐	**b**	a bike.
2 Davina can cook	☐	**c**	pictures.
3 You can speak	☐	**d**	guitar
4 Shirley can play the	☐	**e**	great meals.
5 We can ride	☐	**f**	football.

☐ / 5

Grammar

4 Circle the correct answer.

0 You ___ British!
a isn't (**b**) aren't **c** am not
1 ___ are my T-shirts.
a Those **b** That **c** This
2 Where ___ Clare and Ernie?
a am **b** is **c** are
3 ___ a chair in the bedroom.
a It's **b** They're **c** There's
4 There aren't ___ eggs in the kitchen.
a a **b** an **c** any
5 What ___ got?
a she has **b** have they **c** you have

☐ / 5

5 Circle the correct word.

0 What's *you* / (*your*) favourite colour?
1 *Sean* / *Sean's* dad is a teacher.
2 Ann and I are sisters and Harry is *our* / *his* little brother.
3 The cat is white but *my* / *its* feet are black.
4 *Barbara* / *Barbara's* is a very clever student.
5 I've got two cousins. *Their* / *Her* names are Kelly and Joan.

☐ / 5

6 Complete the text with the words in the box. There is one extra word.

are aren't can got has have ~~is~~

My friend Sarah [0]*is* British. She has [1]__________ two brothers, Bruce and Neil. They [2]__________ very friendly. Sarah is blond but Bruce and Neil [3]__________ got dark hair. They [4]__________ play the guitar but they [5]__________ good at football.

☐ / 5

Vocabulary	☐ / 15	Grammar	☐ / 15
		Your total score	☐ / 30

Get started! Language Test B

name ____________________ class ________

Vocabulary

1 Look at the pictures. Complete the sentences.

0
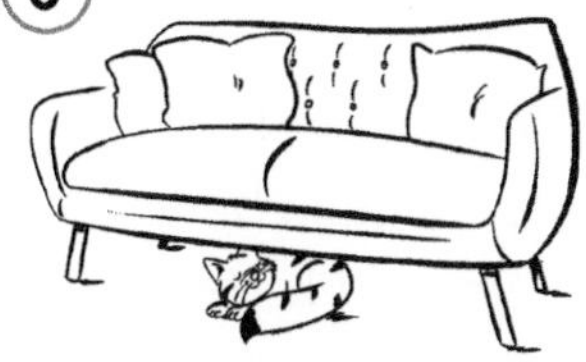

1

2
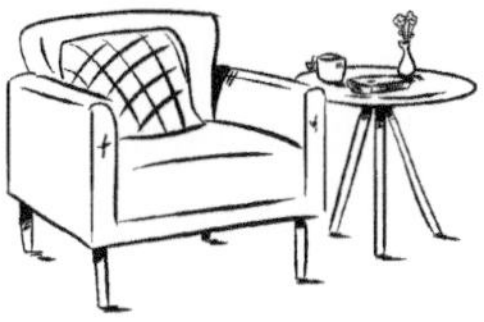

3
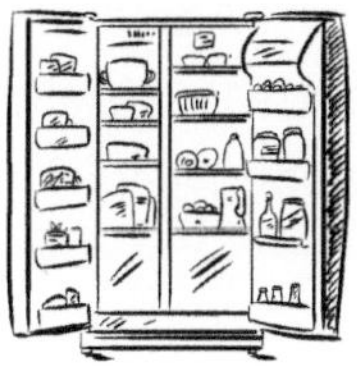

4
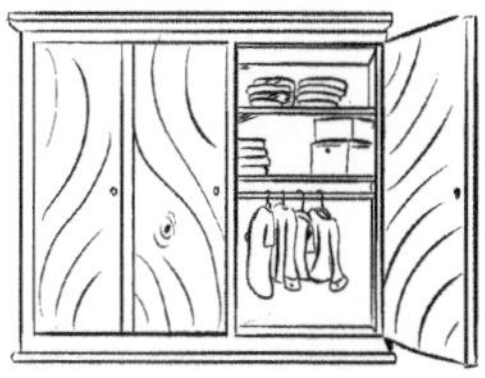

5
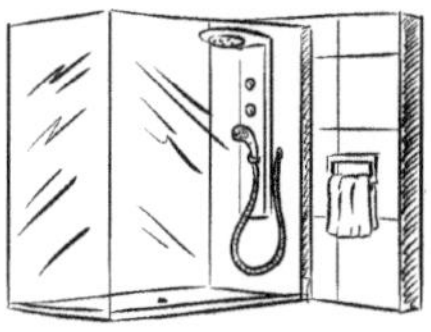

0 The cat is u*nder* the sofa.
1 The books are on the s__________.
2 The table is n__________ t__________ the armchair.
3 The f__________ is in the kitchen.
4 The clothes are in the w__________.
5 The s__________ is in the bathroom.

☐ / 5

2 Find the odd one out.

0	Tuesday	Thursday	(Birthday)	Sunday
1	American	Spain	the UK	Italy
2	Jacket	Jumper	T-shirt	Trousers
3	Small	Helpful	Big	New
4	Argentinian	Chinese	France	Turkish
5	March	Autumn	December	August

☐ / 5

3 Match beginnings 1–5 with endings a–e.

0 Carl can play [*f*]
1 I can sing [ ]
2 Stephen can cook [ ]
3 We can speak [ ]
4 Erica can play the [ ]
5 You can ride [ ]

a lunch for the family.
b Polish.
c English songs.
d piano.
e a horse.
f football.

☐ / 5

Grammar

4 Circle the correct answer.

0 You ___ British!
a isn't (b) aren't c am not
1 There aren't ___ trees in the garden.
a a b an c any
2 ___ are your pencils.
a These b This c That
3 What ___ got?
a have you b he has c they have
4 Ursula ___ got three sisters.
a are b have c has
5 Where ___ Elsa and Frank?
a is b am c are

☐ / 5

5 Circle the correct word.

0 What's *you* / (*your*) favourite colour?
1 The dog is small but *my* / *its* ears are long.
2 The boys in the picture are my cousins. *Their* / *His* names are Jon and Theo.
3 *Zoe* / *Zoe's* is very funny.
4 Charlie and I are brothers and Eva is *our* / *his* little sister.
5 *Paul* / *Paul's* mum is forty-one years old.

☐ / 5

6 Complete the text with the words in the box. There is one extra word.

are are can't got has have ~~is~~

Leslie [0]*is* British. He has [1]__________ two sisters, Laura and Selma. They [2]__________ very nice. Leslie is dark but Laura and Selma [3]__________ got red hair. They [4]__________ skateboard but they [5]__________ good at football.

☐ / 5

Vocabulary	☐ / 15	Grammar	☐ / 15
		Your total score	☐ / 30

1 Language Test A

name ____________________ class ______

Vocabulary

1 Complete the text with missing words.

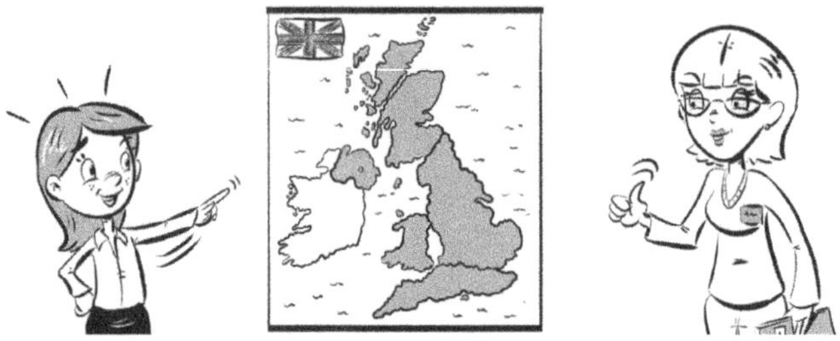

Today is Wednesday. Every Wednesday at nine o'clock we have [0]**F** *r e n c h*. Our teacher comes into the classroom and we say 'Bonjour, Madame Du Bois'. I need my [1]**d** _ _ **t** _ _ **n** _ _ **y** for this lesson. At ten o'clock we have [2]**G** _ _ **g** _ _ **p** _ _. We learn about different countries and we look at [3]**m** _ _ **s**. At eleven we have Maths so I need my [4]**c** _ _ _ **u** _ _ _ **o** _. At twelve we have [5]**S** _ _ **e** _ **c** _, my favourite subject! We do a lot of interesting experiments. In the afternoon, I [6]**p** _ **a** _basketball. Some students [7] _ **o** judo.

☐ / 7

2 Write the names of places in a school.

0 The students have Computer Studies in the **c***omputer* **r***oom*.

1 The teachers and students meet in the **h**__________ every day before lessons start.

2 Everyone has lunch in the school **c**__________.

3 The **s**__________ **r**__________ is for teachers, not students.

4 We do P.E. in the **g**__________.

☐ / 4

Grammar

3 Put the words in the correct order.

0 always / get up / I / on / early / Monday morning

I always get up early on Monday morning.

1 lessons / are / for / late / we / never / Music

____

2 walk / Lucille and Jon / sometimes / school / to

____

3 lunch / you / at / have / home / usually

____

4 with / hang out / often / my friends / I

____

☐ / 4

4 Complete the text with the Present Simple form of the verbs.

My friend Larry

Larry [0]*comes* (come) home from school at half past three. He [1]__________ (have) lunch and then he [2]__________ (do) his homework. He [3]__________ (not watch) TV. Larry has got two sisters, Adele and Frances. Adele is twenty and Frances is nineteen. They [4]__________ (not go) to school. They [5]__________ (work) in a shop.

☐ / 5

5 Complete the dialogues with the words in the box. There is one extra word.

~~do~~ do does she they what yes

A: [0]*Do* you have a History lesson on Tuesdays?
B: [1]__________, I do.

A: [2]__________ Howard listen to music in the evening?
B: No, he plays computer games.

A: [3]__________ Lois and Matt ride their bikes to school?
B: Yes, [4]__________ do.

A: [5]__________ does Samantha do in the evening?
B: She plays chess.

☐ / 5

Communication

6 Complete each dialogue with two words.

0 **A:** What's *your* *name*?
B: Marina Chelsky.

1 **A:** How do you ________ ________?
B: M – A – R – I – N – A, C – H – E – L – S – K – Y.

2 **A:** How old ________ ________?
B: Twelve.

3 **A:** Where do ________ ________?
B: 34 Albany Road, Cambridge.

4 **A:** What's your ________ ________?
B: It's marina190@ynet.com.

5 **A:** What's your ________ ________?
B: 049123456.

☐ / 5

Vocabulary	☐ / 11	Communication	☐ / 5
Grammar	☐ / 14	**Your total score**	☐ / 30

name ______________________ class ________

Vocabulary

1 Complete the text with missing words.

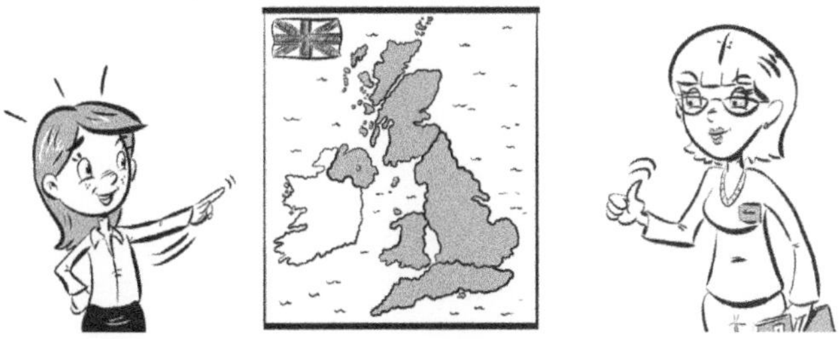

Today is Friday. Every Friday at nine o'clock we have ⁰**F** *r e n c h*. Our teacher comes into the classroom and we say 'Bonjour, Madame Du Bois'. I use my ¹**d** _ _ **t** _ _ **n** _ _ **y** a lot in this lesson. At ten o'clock we have Maths, so I need my ²**c** _ _ _ **u** _ _ _ **o** _. At eleven we have ³**H** _ _ _ **o** _ _, my favourite subject, and we learn about the past. At twelve we have ⁴**G** _ _ **g** _ _ **p** _ _. We learn about different countries and we look at ⁵**m** _ _ **s**. In the afternoon, I ⁶ _ **o** ballet but my friends ⁷**p** _ **a** _ hockey or football.

☐ / [7]

2 Write the names for places in a school.

0 The students have Computer Studies in the **c***omputer* **r***oom*.
1 The **s**________ **r**________ is only for teachers.
2 The students love playing in the **p**________.
3 We often read and study in the **l**________ at school.
4 Everyone has lunch in the school **c**________.

☐ / [4]

Grammar

3 Put the words in the correct order.

0 always / get up / I / on / Monday / early / morning
I always get up early on Monday morning.
1 never / meets / in / his friends / Ken / the park
____
2 the students / home / lunch / usually / at / have
____
3 late / are / for / you / school / sometimes
____
4 often / my friends / school / their bikes / ride / to
____

☐ / [4]

4 Complete the text with the Present Simple form of the verbs.

My Friend Sharon

Sharon ⁰*comes* (come) home from school at four o'clock. She ¹________ (do) her homework and then she ²________ (watch) TV. She ³________ (not play) computer games. Sharon has got two brothers, Tony and Grant. Tony is nineteen and Grant is twenty. They ⁴________ (work) in a shop. They ⁵________ (not go) to school.

☐ / [5]

5 Complete the dialogues with the words in the box. There is one extra word.

~~do~~ do does don't no we what

A: ⁰*Do* you have a Science lesson on Tuesday?
B: ¹________, I don't.

A: ²________ you and your friends walk to school?
B: Yes, ³________ do.

A: ⁴________ does Miles do in the afternoon?
B: He goes skateboarding.

A: ⁵________ your mum cook dinner after work?
B: No, my father cooks dinner.

☐ / [5]

Communication

6 Complete each dialogue with two words.

0 **A:** What's *your name*?
B: Oscar Fuentes.

1 **A:** How do you ________ ________?
B: O – S – C – A – R, F – U – E – N – T – E – S.

2 **A:** How old ________ ________?
B: I'm thirteen years old.

3 **A:** Where do ________ ________?
B: 19 Princess Alexandra Street, Cambridge.

4 **A:** What's your ________ ________?
B: It's oscarxyz@ynet.com.

5 **A:** What's your ________ ________?
B: 081765432.

☐ / [5]

Vocabulary	☐ / [11]	Communication	☐ / [5]
Grammar	☐ / [14]	**Your total score**	☐ / [30]

name   class

Vocabulary

1 Find the odd one out.

0 **Vegetables:** tomatoes / potatoes / (toast)
1 **Fruit:** apples / oranges / pancakes
2 **Food from plants:** cereal / milk / bread
3 **Food from animals:** pasta / ham / meat
4 **Food from the sea:** fish / tuna / yoghurt

◯ / 4

2 Look at the pictures and complete the dialogue.

Owen: Let's look at the menu … The ⁰c_hicken and vegetables look yummy. And I want to try the Chinese ¹r_____. What do you want?

Megan: Hmm. I like chicken, but these ²s_____ look good.

Mimi: Can I have fish and ³c_____?

Megan: Yes, of course!

25 minutes later …

Owen: Are you still hungry?

Mimi: No, but can I have some ⁴s_____?

Owen: Good idea!

Megan: I don't want fruit. I want some ⁵c_____ and biscuits.

Owen: And I want some tea with ⁶s_____.

◯ / 6

3 Write the words for containers in the sentences.

0 Let's buy a p_acket of biscuits for tea.
1 Please buy six c_____ of cola from the supermarket.
2 There's a b_____ of water in the fridge.
3 Is there a j_____ of strawberry jam in the cupboard?
4 There isn't any juice in the c_____.

◯ / 4

Grammar

4 Complete the text with *a/an* or –.

Chocolate mousse

My recipe for chocolate mousse is great! You need ⁰– milk, ¹___ chocolate, ²___ egg, ³___ flour and ⁴___ sugar. You need ⁵___ lemon for the topping too.

◯ / 5

5 Complete the dialogue with the words in the box. There is one extra word.

> a   a lot   any   any   many   much   ~~some~~   some

Izzie: I'm hungry!

Andy: There are ⁰*some* biscuits in the cupboard.

Izzie: How ¹_____ biscuits are there?

Andy: Four.

Izzie: Is there ²_____ carton of apple juice?

Andy: No, there isn't.

Izzie: Is there ³_____ yoghurt?

Andy: No, there isn't, but there's ⁴_____ milk.

Izzie: How ⁵_____ milk is there?

Andy: There's ⁶_____ of milk! We can make milkshakes!

◯ / 6

Communication

6 Put the dialogue in the correct order.

◯ And would you like anything to drink?
◯ Anything else?
1 Are you ready to order? What would you like?
◯ No, thank you.
◯ Yes, please. I'd like a glass of cola, please.
◯ Can I have the pancakes, please?

◯ / 5

Vocabulary ◯ / 14	Communication ◯ / 5
Grammar ◯ / 11	**Your total score** ◯ / 30

2 Language Test B

______________________ name ______ class

Vocabulary

1 Find the odd one out.

0 **Vegetables:** tomatoes / potatoes / (toast)
1 **Food from animals:** ham / pasta / meat
2 **Fruit:** pancakes / apples / oranges
3 **Food from the sea:** tuna / fish / yoghurt
4 **Food from plants:** bread / cereal / milk

☐ / [4]

2 Look at the pictures and complete the dialogue.

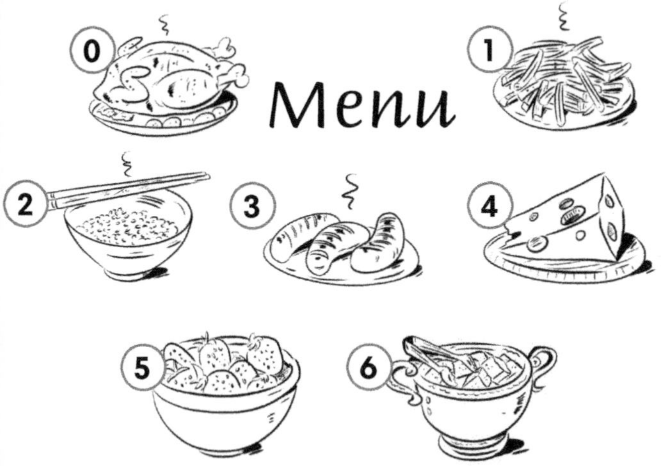

Max: Let's look at the menu … The [0]c*hicken* and vegetables look yummy. And I want some [1]c__________ too. What do you want?
Tanya: Hmm. I like chicken, but I want to try the Chinese [2]r__________.
Sonia: Can I have the [3]s__________?
Tanya: Yes, of course!
25 minutes later …
Max: Are you still hungry?
Sonia: Yes, I am! Can I have some [4]c__________ and biscuits now?
Max: Good idea!
Tanya: I want some [5]s__________ and cream.
Max: And I want some coffee with [6]s__________.

☐ / [6]

3 Write the words for containers in the sentences.

0 Let's buy a p*acket* of biscuits for tea.
1 I'd like that b__________ of chocolate, please.
2 Let's buy a j__________ of jam from the supermarket.
3 There's a b__________ of water in the kitchen.
4 There are four c__________ of cola in the fridge.

☐ / [4]

Grammar

4 Complete the text with *a/an* or –.

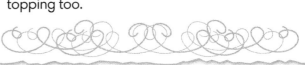

Chocolate mousse

My recipe for chocolate mousse is great! You need [0]– milk, [1]__ egg, [2]__ chocolate, [3]__ flour and [4]__ sugar. You need [5]__ lemon for the topping too.

☐ / [5]

5 Complete the dialogue with the words in the box. There is one extra word.

a lot an any any many much ~~some~~ some

Lilian: I'm hungry!
Nigel: There's [0]*some* bread in the kitchen.
Lilian: How [1]__________ bread is there?
Nigel: There's [2]__________ of bread.
Lilian: Good! We can make [3]__________ sandwiches.
Nigel: Is there [4]__________ butter?
Andy: No, there isn't, so we can't make [5]__________ sandwiches. But look! Biscuits!
Lilian: How [6]__________ biscuits are there?
Nigel: One, two, three, … nine!
Lilian: Let's eat!

☐ / [6]

Communication

6 Put the dialogue in the correct order.

☐ Anything else?
☐ And would you like anything to drink?
☐ No, thank you.
☐ Yes, please. I'd like a glass of juice, please.
☐ Can I have a pizza, please?
[1] Are you ready to order? What would you like?

☐ / [5]

Vocabulary	☐ / [14]	Communication	☐ / [5]
Grammar	☐ / [11]	**Your total score**	☐ / [30]

name ______________________ class ________

Vocabulary

1 Complete the text with missing words.

Young people love technology. We can't live without it! We love taking [0]**s** _e_ **l** _f_ _i_ _e_ **s** with our mobile phones. We [1]**t** _ _ **k** on the phone a lot too. My friends and I have a computer at home: some people have got a laptop too, and other people have got a [2]**t** _ _ **l** _ _. We never buy CDs. We always [3]**d** _ _ _ **l** _ _ _ songs and we use our [4]**h** _ _ _ **p** _ _ _ **e** _ to listen to music. We sometimes [5]**s** _ **n** _ emails but we usually [6]**t** _ _ **t** our friends or we chat [7]**o** _ _ **i** _ _.
What's your favourite item of technology?

☐ / [7]

2 Circle the correct word.

0 I've got a new laptop! I'm (*happy*) / *scared* / *tired*.
1 I'm not *interested* / *scared* / *good* at fixing things, but my brother is fantastic.
2 Are you *bad* / *bored* / *interested* in technology?
3 Angela is *excited* / *scared* / *angry* of big dogs.
4 Lee works all day so he feels *tired* / *excited* / *interested* in the evening.
5 The children are *scared* / *interested* / *worried* about their mum. She looks sad.

☐ / [5]

Grammar

3 Use the Present Continuous form of the verbs. Write short forms when you can.

Hi, Granny! … Yes, we're all fine. … I [0]*'m sitting* (sit) in the garden. Mum and Dad are in the living room. … No, they [1]______________ (not watch) TV. Dad [2]______________ (write) emails and Mum [3]______________ (listen) to music. … What [4]______________ (I / do)? I [5]______________ (surf) the Internet. What about you?

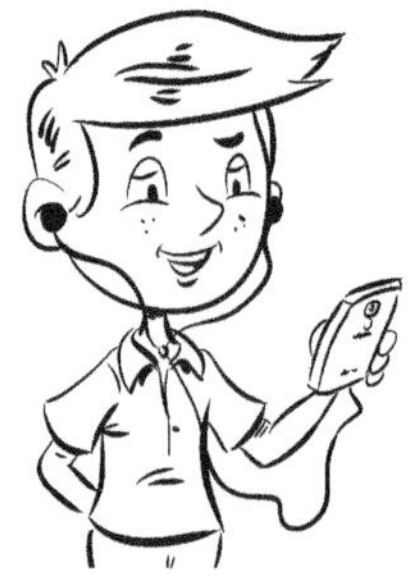

☐ / [5]

4 Complete the dialogues.

0 **A:** Are Billy and Marcus chatting with their friends?
B: Yes, *they are*.

1 **A:** Are you playing a good computer game?
B: No, ______________.

2 **A:** Is your teacher standing in front of the board?
B: Yes, ______________.

3 **A:** Are you and your sister having lunch?
B: No, ______________.

4 **A:** Are the students going to the canteen?
B: Yes, ______________.

☐ / [4]

5 Complete the questions.

0 **A:** Where is *your dad going*?
B: My dad is going to work.

1 **A:** What is ______________________?
B: Roxanne is driving a lorry.

2 **A:** Why are ______________________ to bed?
B: I am going to bed because it's late.

3 **A:** Are ______________________ on the carpet?
B: Yes, the cats are sleeping on the carpet.

4 **A:** What are ______________________?
B: The students are reading their books.

☐ / [4]

Communication

6 Complete the dialogue with one word in each gap.

Seth: Hello, Mrs Carter. It's Seth [0]**h***ere*.
Mrs Carter: Oh, hello, Seth. How are you?
Seth: [1]**F**_________, thanks. Can I [2]**s**_________ to Ollie, [3]**p**_________?
Mrs Carter: [4]**H**_________ on, please. Ollie! Ollie! It's Seth for you.
Ollie: Hi, Seth.
Seth: Hi, Ollie. Do you want to come to my house and watch a DVD?
Ollie: Great idea. See you [5]**s**_________.

☐ / [5]

Vocabulary	☐ / [12]	Communication	☐ / [5]
Grammar	☐ / [13]	**Your total score**	☐ / [30]

3 Language Test B

name ______________________ class ______

Vocabulary

1 Complete the text with missing words.

Young people love technology. We can't live without it! We love taking **⁰s** _e_ **l** _f i e_ **s** with our mobile phones. We **¹s** _ **r** _ the Internet a lot too. My friends and I have a computer at home: some people have got a tablet too, and other people have got a **²l** _ _ **t** _ _.
We usually **³d** _ _ _ **l** _ _ _ songs and we use our **⁴h** _ _ _ **p** _ _ _ **e** _ to listen to music.
We sometimes **⁵s** _ **n** _ emails but we usually **⁶t** _ _ **t** our friends or we **⁷c** _ _ **t** online.

[ ] / [7]

2 Circle the correct word.

0 I've got a new laptop! I'm *(happy)* / *scared* / *tired.*
1 Barry is *angry* / *excited* / *scared* of big dogs!
2 I am *interested* / *worried* / *scared* about my friend. He looks sad.
3 Are you *interested* / *bad* / *bored* in Science and Technology?
4 Sandra isn't *interested* / *scared* / *good* at playing chess, but her brother is fantastic.
5 Paul works all week so he feels *excited* / *tired* / *interested* at the weekend.

[ ] / [5]

Grammar

3 Use the Present Continuous form of the verbs. Write short forms when you can.

Hi, Granny! … Yes, we're all fine. … I ⁰*'m sitting* (sit) in the garden. … Bert? Oh, Bert ¹__________ (do) his homework in his bedroom. And Mum, Uncle Darren and Aunt Vicky are in the living room. They ²__________ (talking). … No, Dad ³__________ (not watch) TV. He ⁴__________ (sing) in the shower. I can hear him! What ⁵__________ (you / do)?

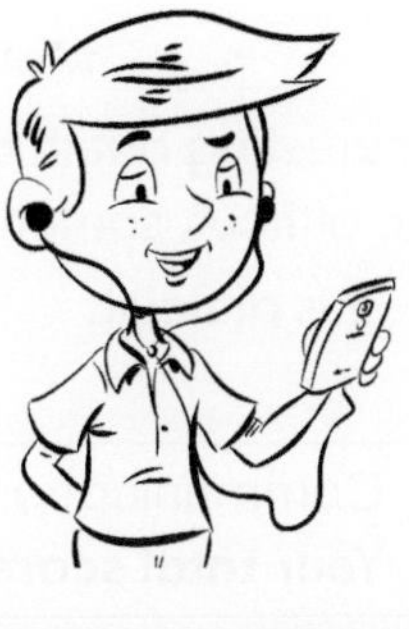

[ ] / [5]

4 Complete the dialogues.

0 **A:** Are Billy and Marcus chatting with their friends?
B: Yes, *they are*.

1 **A:** Is Jenny going to the library?
B: No, __________.

2 **A:** Are you and your family having dinner?
B: Yes, __________.

3 **A:** Is the boy listening to music?
B: Yes, __________.

4 **A:** Are Ian and Vanessa studying for a test?
B: No, __________.

[ ] / [4]

5 Complete the questions.

0 **A:** Where is *your dad going*?
B: My dad is going to work.

1 **A:** Are __________ in the staff room?
B: No, the teachers aren't sitting in the staff room.

2 **A:** What __________?
B: Louisa is drinking orange juice.

3 **A:** Why are __________ home?
B: Kate and I are going home because it's late.

4 **A:** Where are __________?
B: The little girls are playing in the garden.

[ ] / [4]

Communication

6 Complete the dialogue with one word in each gap.

Simon: Hello, Mrs Winters. It's Simon **⁰h***ere*.
Mrs Winters: Hello, Simon. How are you?
Simon: I'm **¹f**__________, thanks. Can I **²s**__________ to Gabriella, **³p**__________?
Mrs Winters: **⁴J**______ a minute. Gabriella! It's Simon for you.
Gabriella: Hi, Simon.
Simon: Hi, Gabriella. Do you want to go skateboarding with me?
Gabriella: That's a good idea. See you **⁵l**__________.

[ ] / [5]

Vocabulary	[ ] / [12]	Communication	[ ] / [5]
Grammar	[ ] / [13]	**Your total score**	[ ] / [30]

4 Language Test A

name ______________________ class ________

Vocabulary

1 Write the names of places. Use the map to help you.

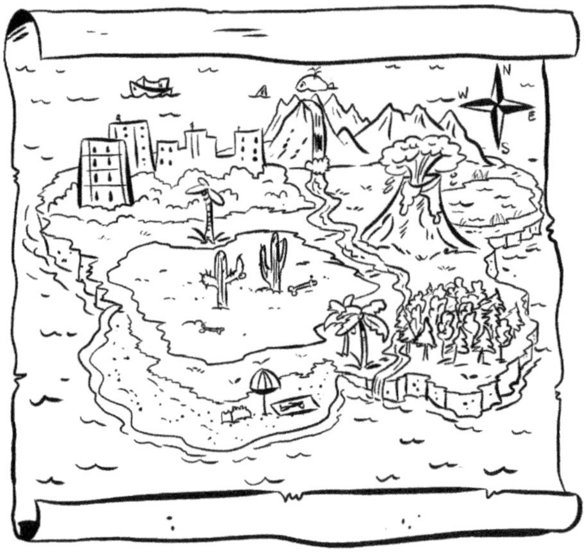

0 It is thousands of metres high. People sometimes climb it. *mountain*
1 It is big. There are thousands of houses and a lot of people live there. ______________
2 It has got thousands of trees. ______________
3 There aren't any trees here. It is very hot and it doesn't often rain. ______________
4 It is next to the sea. People sit on it under umbrellas. ______________
5 It is hundreds of kilometres long. It is full of water and fish live in it. ______________
6 You can come here in a boat. You can't walk or drive here. ______________
7 It is a kind of mountain. It is very dangerous. ______________

☐ / [7]

2 Complete the sentences with the adjectives in the box. There is one extra word.

beautiful boring ~~difficult~~ exciting expensive kind low

0 I can't do this exercise. It's too *difficult*.
1 Look at the flowers! They are ______________ .
2 Nathan is a nice boy. He's ______________ to people and he helps them.
3 You can't buy this T-shirt. It's too ______________ !
4 This film isn't interesting. It's ______________ .
5 The wall is only one metre high. It's a ______________ wall.

☐ / [5]

Grammar

3 Use the comparative form of the adjectives.

0 *cold cities*: Moscow** / London*
Moscow *is colder than* London.
1 *high mountains*: Mount Olympus** / Mount Rysy*
Mount Olympus ______________ Mount Rysy.
2 *big animals*: tigers** / cats*
Tigers ______________ cats.
3 *good films*: *The Lion King*** / *Madagascar**
The Lion King ______________ *Madagascar*.
4 *dangerous animals*: sharks** / rats*
Sharks ______________ rats.
5 *easy questions*: question 2** / question 7*
Question 2 ______________ question 7.

☐ / [5]

4 Use the superlative form of the adjectives.

0 The Pacific is *the biggest* (big) ocean in the world.
1 I've got ______________ (curly) hair in the class.
2 Is the Sahara ________ (hot) desert in the world?
3 Mr May is ________ (good) teacher in the school.
4 I think golf is ________ (boring) sport in the world.

☐ / [4]

5 Use one word in each gap in the sentences.

0 I think windsurfing is *more* exciting than sailing.
1 Who is ________ funniest actor in the world?
2 History is ________ interesting than Geography.
3 What is the ________ beautiful bird in the world?
4 The pizza is nicer ________ the pasta.

☐ / [4]

Communication

6 Use the words in the box in the dialogue. There is one extra word.

about of opinion right think ~~what's~~ wrong

A: [0]*What's* your favourite subject at school?
B: Science. What [1]__________ you?
A: I like Science, but my favourite subject is English.
B: What do you think [2]__________ Maths?
A: I [3]__________ it's interesting but in my [4]__________, it's too difficult sometimes.
B: You're [5]__________. It is difficult.

☐ / [5]

Vocabulary	☐ / [12]	Communication	☐ / [5]
Grammar	☐ / [13]	**Your total score**	☐ / [30]

Language Test B

name ______________________ class ______

Vocabulary

1 Write the names of places. Use the map to help you.

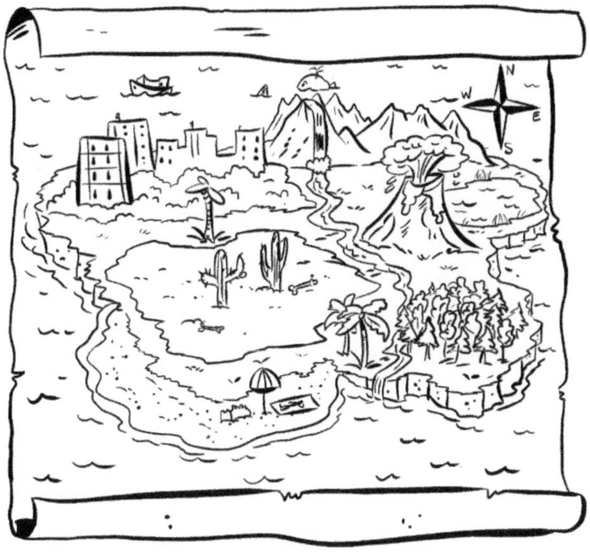

0 It is thousands of metres high. People sometimes climb it. *mountain*
1 It is very hot here and it doesn't often rain. It hasn't got any trees. ______
2 Fish live in it. It is hundreds of kilometres long. ______
3 It is a very dangerous mountain. ______
4 There are a lot of houses and streets in this place. A lot of people live here. ______
5 People like sitting here in the summer. It is next to the sea. ______
6 You can't walk or drive to get here but you can come here in a boat. ______
7 There are thousands of trees here. ______

[ ] / [7]

2 Complete the sentences with the adjectives in the box. There is one extra word.

beautiful boring cheap ~~difficult~~ exciting kind low

0 I can't do this exercise. It's too *difficult*.
1 The wall is ______ . It's only a metre high.
2 The birds in the zoo are ______ . They've got fantastic colours!
3 Golf is a(n) ______ sport. We always watch it on TV.
4 These jeans are £50! They aren't ______ !
5 Nancy is a friendly girl. She helps people and she's ______ to them.

[ ] / [5]

Grammar

3 Use the comparative form of the adjectives.

0 ***cold** countries*: Russia** / the UK*
Russia *is colder than* the UK.
1 ***bad** cafés*: Pete's Café** / The Ivy Café*
Pete's Café ______ The Ivy Café.
2 ***expensive** cities*: New York** / Budapest*
New York ______ Budapest.
3 ***cute** animals*: puppies** / parrots*
Puppies ______ parrots.
4 ***fast** animals*: zebras** / cats*
Zebras ______ cats.
5 ***easy** languages*: English**/ Chinese*
English ______ Chinese.

[ ] / [5]

4 Use the superlative form of the adjectives.

0 The Pacific is *the biggest* (big) ocean in the world.
1 I think football is ______ (boring) sport.
2 He's got ______ (curly) hair in the class.
3 Mrs Fry is ______ (good) teacher in the school.
4 Is the Gobi ______ (hot) desert in the world?

[ ] / [4]

5 Use one word in each gap in the sentences.

0 I think windsurfing is *more* exciting than sailing.
1 This dress is prettier ______ that one.
2 Who is ______ best actor in the world?
3 Anne is the ______ beautiful girl in my class.
4 Music is ______ interesting than Science.

[ ] / [4]

Communication

6 Use the words in the box in the dialogue. There is one extra word.

favourite in right think ~~what's~~ wrong you

A: [0]*What's* your favourite subject at school?
B: History. What about [1]______?
A: I like History but my [2]______ subject is French.
B: What do you [3]______ of Science?
A: It's great but [4]______ my opinion, it's too difficult.
B: You're [5]______. It is difficult.

[ ] / [5]

Vocabulary	[ ] / [12]	Communication	[ ] / [5]
Grammar	[ ] / [13]	**Your total score**	[ ] / [30]

5 Language Test A

name ______________________ class ________

Vocabulary

1 Write the names of places in a town.

0 Where can you watch a film? **c***inema*

1 Where can you send a postcard or a letter?
p__________ **o**__________

2 Where can you stay when you are on holiday?
h__________

3 Where can you dive and swim? **s**__________
p__________

4 Where can you get money? **b**__________

5 Where do doctors work? **h**__________

6 Where can you have dinner? **r**__________

7 Where can you watch actors? **t**__________

___ / [7]

2 Look at the picture and complete the text with the words in the box.

behind	between	~~in front of~~	next to	opposite

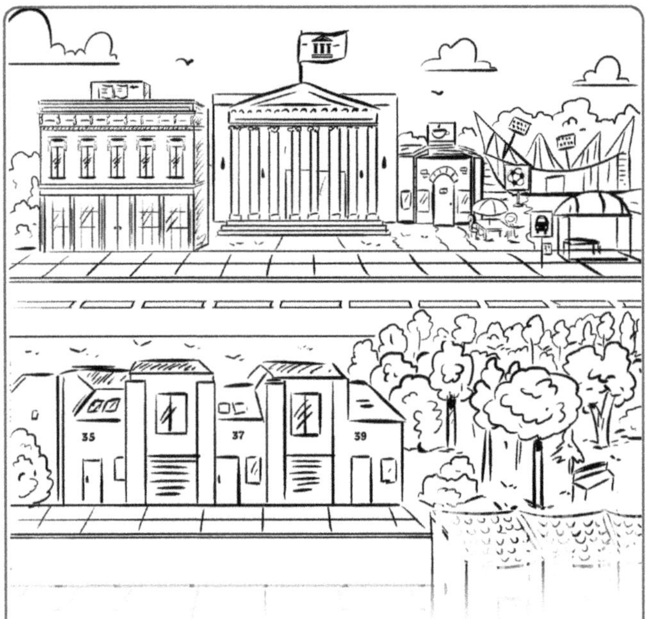

My town — by Maryanne Robinson

In my town, there's a great football stadium. There's a bus stop [0]*in front of* the stadium. I often watch football matches there. There's a cool café [1]______________ the stadium. The museum is [2]______________ the café and the library. There's a small park [3]______________ the café. [4]______________ the park there's a street with houses. I live there, at number 39.

___ / [4]

3 Complete the text with adjectives.

My town — by Vinnie Smith

I don't live in a big city. I live in a [0]**s***mall* town. Big cities are dirty but my town is [1]**c**__________. The houses here aren't old. They're [2]**m**__________. The streets are busy in the morning and afternoon, but at night they're [3]**q**__________. Some people think my town is boring but they're wrong. You can do a lot of [4]**i**__________ activities here.

___ / [4]

Grammar

4 Use the correct Past Simple form of *be*: affirmative [✓] or negative [✗].

0 I am happy today but I *was* sad yesterday. ✓

1 Why ______ you at home last night? ✗

2 Martha ______ in London in 2015. ✓

3 There ______ some people in the park last night. ✓

4 The children ______ at school last week. ✗

5 There ______ any milk in the fridge yesterday. ✗

___ / [5]

5 Complete the dialogues with the words in the box. There is one extra word.

no	there	~~was~~	was	wasn't	weren't	yes

A: Tell me about the party yesterday. [0]*Was* James there?

B: [1]________, he was, but Doreen and Michael [2]________ there. They're on holiday.

A: Were [3]________ a lot of people?

B: No, but it [4]________ a good party. It [5]________ very boring!

___ / [5]

Communication

6 Use one word in each gap in the dialogue.

A: [0]**E***xcuse* me. I'm looking for Newtown Bank.

B: Oh yes. I know where that is. It's [1]**o**________ Green Street.

A: Where's Green Street? Is it [2]**f**________?

B: No, it isn't. Go [3]**s**________ on, then turn left. Go [4]**p**________ the library and the bank is on the [5]**r**________.

A: Thank you.

___ / [5]

Vocabulary	___ / [15]	Communication	___ / [5]
Grammar	___ / [10]	**Your total score**	___ / [30]

5 Language Test B

name ______________________ class ________

Vocabulary

1 Write the names of places in a town.

0 Where can you watch a film? **c**_inema_
1 Where do doctors work? **h**__________
2 Where can you get money? **b**__________
3 Where can you go to read books and use a computer? **l**__________
4 Where can you have dinner? **r**__________
5 Where can you watch actors? **t**__________
6 Where can you stay when you are on holiday? **h**__________
7 Where can you send a postcard or a letter? **p**__________ **o**__________

☐ / 7

2 Look at the picture and complete the text with the words in the box.

behind   between   ~~in front of~~   next to   opposite

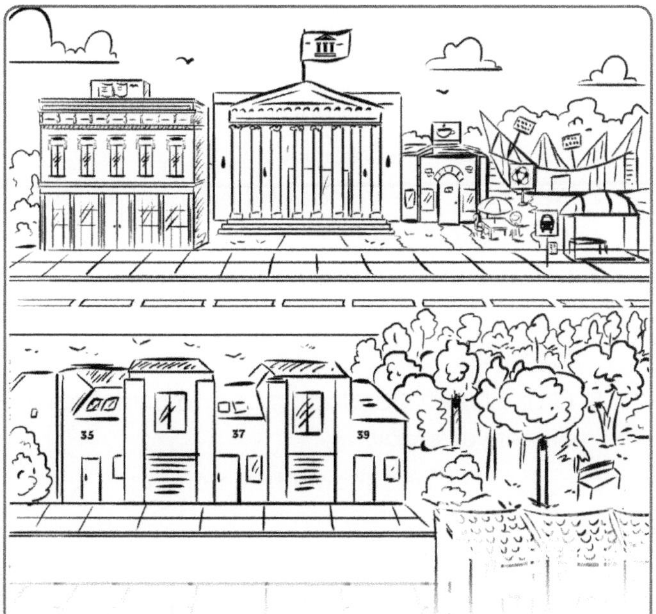

My town *by William Clarke*

In my town, there's a great football stadium. There's a bus stop [0] _in front of_ the stadium. My family and I often watch football matches there. There's also a cool café. It's [1] __________ the stadium and the museum. The town library is [2] __________ the museum. There's a park [3] __________ the café and the stadium. There's a street with houses [4] __________ the park. We live there, at number 35.

☐ / 4

3 Complete the text with adjectives.

My town *by Harriet Cameron*

I don't live in a small town. I live in a [0] **b**_ig_ city. Small towns are usually clean but cities are often [1] **d**__________. The houses in my city aren't [2] **m**__________. They're old. The streets are [3] **b**__________ in the morning, afternoon and evening. They're never quiet. The city has got a lot of problems but it's always interesting. It's never [4] **b**__________!

☐ / 4

Grammar

4 Use the correct Past Simple form of *be*: affirmative [✓] or negative [✗].

0 I am happy today but I _was_ sad yesterday. ✓
1 There ______ some people in the street last Friday. ✓
2 Morris ______ well last week. ✓
3 Anya and Otto ______ in Madrid in 2009. ✗
4 There ______ some eggs in the shop yesterday. ✓
5 Mum ______ at home last night. ✗

☐ / 5

5 Complete the dialogues with the words in the box. There is one extra word.

no   there   ~~was~~   was   wasn't   were   yes

A: Tell me about the party yesterday. [0] _Was_ Tim there?
B: [1] __________, he wasn't. He's on holiday but Haley and Steve [2] __________ there.
A: Were [3] __________ a lot of people?
B: Yes, it [4] __________ a fantastic party! It [5] __________ boring!

☐ / 5

Communication

6 Use one word in each gap in the dialogue.

A: [0] **E**_xcuse_ me. I'm looking for the library.
B: Oh yes. I know where that is. It's [1] **o**__________ Lord Roberts Street.
A: Is it [2] **f**__________?
B: No, it isn't. Go [3] **s**__________ on, then turn right. Go [4] **p**__________ the cinema and the library is on the [5] **l**__________.
A: Thank you.

☐ / 5

Vocabulary	☐ / 15	Communication	☐ / 5
Grammar	☐ / 10	**Your total score**	☐ / 30

6 Language Test A

name ______________________ class ______

Vocabulary

1 Write the names of jobs. Use the pictures to help you.

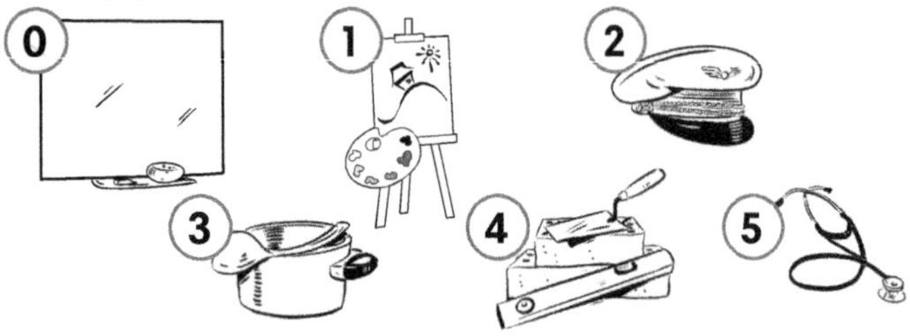

0 This person works in a school. *t e a c h e r*
1 This person paints pictures. _ _ _ _ _ _
2 This person flies a plane. _ _ _ _ _
3 This person cooks food in a restaurant. _ _ _ _
4 This person makes houses and walls. _ _ _ _ _ _ _
5 This person works with ill pets. _ _ _

__ / 5

2 Complete the sentences.

0 Marco drives a bus. He's a **b***us* **d***river*.
1 Marilyn sings in a musical. She's a **s**_________.
2 Suzette works in an office. She's an **o**_________ **w**_________.
3 Brandon looks after ill people in a hospital. He's a **n**_________ .
4 Lucille helps customers in a shop. She's a **s**_________ **a**_________.

__ / 4

3 Choose the correct answer.

Good morning, kids!
Please do these jobs before you go out.
Jimmy, please [0]__ the shopping. The shopping list is on the fridge door. And [1]__ the bin in the kitchen. It's full!
Sonia, please [2]__ the dishes – and [3]__ the dog. He needs exercise!
Finally, Jimmy AND Sonia: [4]__ your beds and tidy your rooms! What a mess they are!
Love, Mum

0	a make	(b) do	c have
1	a empty	b take	c try
2	a watch	b feel	c wash
3	a take	b walk	c go
4	a do	b clean	c make

__ / 4

Grammar

4 Write the Past Simple form of the verbs in the text.

Hi Bob,

Let me tell you about yesterday. I [0]*visited* (visit) my cousins Alex and Dan. I [1]_________ (arrive) at their house at ten o'clock. Alex and I [2]_________ (play) chess for an hour. Then Dan [3]_________ (make) some pancakes for lunch. We [4]_________ (want) to go to the park in the afternoon but it was rainy. The rain [5]_________ (stop) at five o'clock and then I [6]_________ (go) home.

How was your day? Lewis

__ / 6

5 Write the Past Simple form of the verbs in the box.

come ~~drink~~ have live meet take try

0 Yesterday I *drank* orange juice for breakfast.
1 Henry _______ some photos on his holiday.
2 We _______ our friends at the shopping centre last Saturday.
3 I _______ in Spain when I was six years old.
4 Maria _______ to study for her test but she was too tired.
5 Granny and Grandad _______ to our house for dinner yesterday.
6 I _______ a long shower this morning.

__ / 6

Communication

6 Use one word in each gap in the dialogue.

A: Oh no! I can't find my ruler! Can I [0]**b***orrow* your ruler?
B: [1]**S**_______, no problem.

A: Is it OK [2]**i**_______ I use your mobile phone?
B: Yes, that's [3]**f**_______.

A: Can I use your laptop, [4]**p**_______? I want to send an email.
B: No, [5]**s**_______, you can't. I'm using it.

__ / 5

Vocabulary	__ / 13	Communication	__ / 5
Grammar	__ / 12	**Your total score**	__ / 30

6 Language Test B

name ______________________ class ________

Vocabulary

1 Write the names of jobs. Use the pictures to help you.

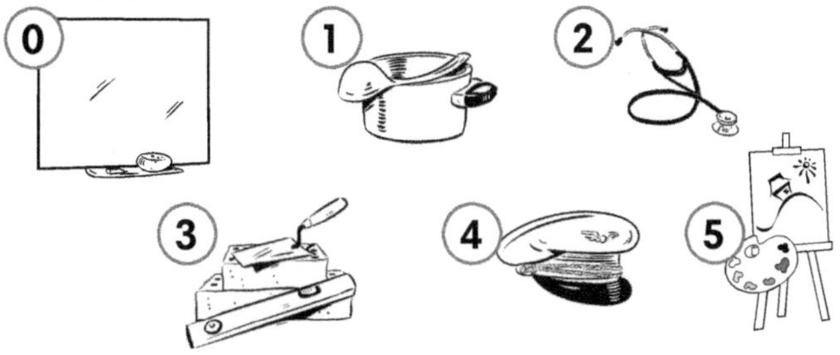

0 This person works in a school. *t e a c h e r*
1 This person cooks food in a restaurant. _ _ _ _
2 This person works with ill pets. _ _ _
3 This person makes houses and walls. _ _ _ _ _ _ _ _
4 This person flies a plane. _ _ _ _ _
5 This person paints pictures. _ _ _ _ _ _

☐ / 5

2 Complete the sentences.

0 Marco drives a bus. He's a **b***us* **d***river*.
1 Nigel looks after ill people. He's a **n**__________ .
2 Peggy sings in a theatre. She's a **s**__________.
3 Lucille helps customers in a shop. She's a **s**__________ **a**__________.
4 Simon works in an office. He's an **o**__________ **w**__________.

☐ / 4

3 Choose the correct answer.

Good morning, kids!
Please do these jobs before you go out.
Adam, please ⁰__ the shopping. The shopping list is on the fridge door. And ¹__ after your little brother!
Gillian, please ²__ the bin in the kitchen. It's full! And ³__ the car. It's very dirty.
Finally, Adam AND Gillian: ⁴__ your room and make your beds! What a mess they are!
Love, Mum

0	**a** make	[**b**] do	**c** have
1	**a** see	**b** watch	**c** look
2	**a** take	**b** make	**c** empty
3	**a** wash	**b** watch	**c** do
4	**a** do	**b** tidy	**c** wash

☐ / 4

Grammar

4 Write the Past Simple form of the verbs in the text.

Hi Kiki,

Let me tell you about last week. I ⁰*visited* (visit) my cousins Vivian and Terry. I ¹__________ (go) to their house at eleven o'clock. Vivian and I ²__________ (listen) to music for an hour. Then Terry ³__________ (make) pizza for lunch. We ⁴__________ (want) to go to the swimming pool in the afternoon but it was rainy. The rain ⁵__________ (stop) at five o'clock and then I ⁶__________ (walk) home.

How was your day? Alice

☐ / 6

5 Write the Past Simple form of the verbs in the box.

ask come ~~drink~~ eat have take try

0 Yesterday I *drank* a glass of orange juice for breakfast.
1 I ______ Dad for some money yesterday.
2 We ______ a cool Maths lesson last Wednesday.
3 The children ______ ham and cheese sandwiches for lunch.
4 You ______ a lot of photos on your holiday!
5 My aunt ______ to our house last Monday.
6 I ______ to do my homework but it wasn't easy.

☐ / 6

Communication

6 Use one word in each gap in the dialogue.

A: Oh no! I can't find my ruler! Can I ⁰**b***orrow* your ruler?
B: Oh, ¹**a**_______ right.

A: Is it OK ²**i**_______ I use your dictionary?
B: Sure, no ³**p**_______.

A: Can I use your tablet, ⁴**p**_______? I want to surf the Internet.
B: No, ⁵**s**_______, you can't. I'm using it.

☐ / 5

Vocabulary	☐ / 13	Communication	☐ / 5
Grammar	☐ / 12	**Your total score**	☐ / 30

© Pearson Education Limited 2017 PHOTOCOPIABLE

name ______________________ class ______

Vocabulary

1 Complete the text with the words in the box.

arrive ~~bike~~ leaves motorbike on takes underground

I love cycling and I go to school by [0]*bike*. My best friend goes [1]__________ foot. I usually [2]__________ at school before he does. Mum [3]__________ a bus to work. She [4]__________ home ten past eight in the morning. Dad travels to work by [5]__________. He likes it because he can read his newspaper then. My big sister goes everywhere by [6]__________. She loves riding it!

☐ / 6

2 Look at the pictures and complete the text.

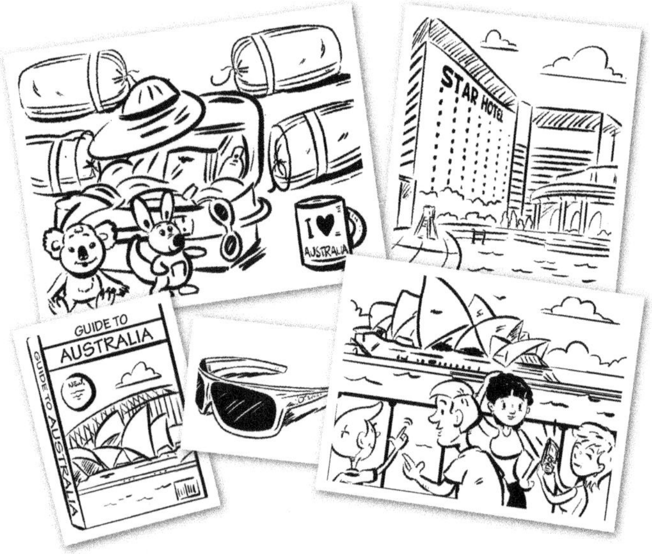

Hi Felicity,
Guess what! We're back home! We had a FANTASTIC holiday in Australia! Dad bought a [0]g*uidebook* and we went [1]s__________ in Sydney. We stayed in a great [2]h__________.
I bought [3]s__________ – it was very sunny!
Then we went camping in the Blue Mountains, so we took our [4]s__________ b__________. My [5]s__________ was heavy when we came back because I bought a lot of [6]s__________. The toy kangaroo is for you! And I've got a lot of photos to show you!!
See you soon. Cassandra

☐ / 6

Grammar

3 Use the Past Simple form of the verbs in the text.

Dad and Aunt Cindy [0]*didn't have* (not have) holidays like us when they were children. They [1]__________ (not take) a lot of photos. Dad [2]__________ (not watch) TV and Aunt Cindy [3]__________ (not surf) the Internet. Dad says: 'We [4]__________ (not use) technology but we [5]__________ (have) a lot of fun.'

☐ / 5

4 Write questions and short answers.

A: I bought some new clothes yesterday.
B: [0]*Did you buy* a dress?
A: No, [0]*I didn't*. I bought a hoodie.

A: Thomas ate lunch at this café yesterday.
B: [1]__________ a sandwich?
B: Yes, [2]__________.

A: Mum and Dad cooked dinner last night.
B: [3]__________ pasta?
A: No, [4]__________. They cooked pizza.

☐ / 4

5 Complete the questions.

A: [0]Did *you have fun* on your holiday?
B: Yes, we had a lot of fun.
A: [1]Where did __________________?
B: We went to Spain.
A: [2]How did __________________ there?
B: We travelled there by plane.
A: [3]Did __________________ Granada?
B: No, we didn't see Granada.
A: [4]When did __________________ home?
B: I came home last Saturday.

☐ / 4

Communication

6 Put the dialogue in the correct order.

[ ] What time does the train leave?
[1] I'd like a ticket to Manchester, please.
[ ] At ten minutes to eight.
[ ] Here you are.
[7] Thanks.
[ ] How much is it?
[ ] It's seventy-five pounds, please.

☐ / 5

Vocabulary	☐ / 12	Communication	☐ / 5
Grammar	☐ / 13	**Your total score**	☐ / 30

name _____   class _____

Vocabulary

1 Complete the text with the words in the box.

arrive ~~bike~~ bus leave motorbike on take

My best friend goes to school by ⁰*bike*. I don't like cycling, so I go there ¹_____ foot. Mum and Dad ²_____ the train to work. They usually ³_____ home at ten past eight and they go to the train station by ⁴_____. They ⁵_____ at work at ten to nine. My big brother goes everywhere by ⁶_____ . He loves riding it!

☐ / ⑥

2 Look at the pictures and complete the text.

Hi Matt,

We're back home! We had a FANTASTIC holiday in Australia! We bought a ⁰*guidebook* and we went ¹s_____ in Sydney. Then we went to the Blue Mountains. We didn't stay in a ²h_____ . We went camping so we took our ³s _____ b_____. I bought a lot of ⁴s_____ in Australia so my ⁵s_____ was heavy. The toy koala is for you. I bought ⁶s_____ – it was sunny every day! And I've got a lot of photos to show you when I see you.

Bye for now.   Nicky

☐ / ⑥

Grammar

3 Use the Past Simple form of the verbs in the text.

Mum and Uncle Chris ⁰*didn't have* (not have) holidays like us when they were children. They ¹_____ (not text) their friends. Mum ²_____ (not chat) with her friends online and Uncle Chris ³_____ (not watch) DVDs on his tablet. Mum says: 'We ⁴_____ (not use) technology but we ⁵_____ (have) a lot of fun.'

☐ / ⑤

4 Write questions and short answers.

A: I bought some new clothes yesterday.
B: ⁰*Did you buy* a dress?
A: No,⁰*I didn't*. I bought a hoodie.
   A: Sharon tidied the house last Saturday.
   B: ¹_____ the kitchen?
   A: Yes, ²_____ .
A: Heather and Malcolm ate dinner at an Italian restaurant last week.
B: ³_____ pasta?
A: No, ⁴_____ . The ate pizza.

☐ / ④

5 Complete the questions.

A: ⁰Did *you have fun* on your holiday?
B: Yes, I had a lot of fun.
A: ¹Where did _____?
B: I travelled <u>to Germany</u>.
A: ²How did _____ there?
B: We went there <u>by train</u>.
A: ³Did you _____ the Rhine?
B: <u>Yes</u>, we saw the Rhine.
A: ⁴When did _____ home?
B: I came home <u>yesterday</u>.

☐ / ④

Communication

6 Put the dialogue in the correct order.

☐ It's thirty pounds fifty, please.
☐ What time does the train leave?
☐ Here you are.
⑦ Thanks.
① I'd like a ticket to Bristol, please.
☐ How much is it?
☐ At three minutes past five.

☐ / ⑤

Vocabulary ☐ / ⑫		Communication ☐ / ⑤	
Grammar ☐ / ⑬		**Your total score** ☐ / ㉚	

49

8 Language Test A

name ______________________ class ________

Vocabulary

1 Write the names of events.

0 People celebrate a special day.
a b*irthda***y party**
1 Children go to a friend's house and sleep there. **a s**___________**r**
2 People act, sing or dance and the best person wins. **a talent c**___________**n**
3 People cook meat and sausages in the garden. **a b**___________**e**
4 People go to the theatre and watch actors act. **a p**___________**y**
5 People take food with them and have lunch in the park or on a beach. **a p**___________**c**
6 People wear a costume and have fun together.
a f___________**y d**___________**s party**

▢ / 6

2 Write the types of music and dates.

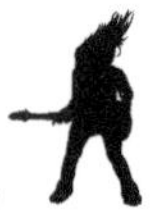
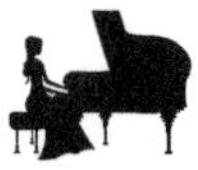
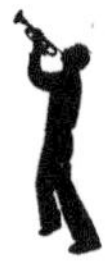

A: There are great concerts in our town this year.
B: Cool! I'd love to go to the [0]r *o c k* concert. When is it?
A: It's on [0]*the third of April*. (3.04)
B: OK. When is the [1]r _ _ _ _ _ concert?
A: It's on [2]___________________. (15.01)
B: Great! Hmm. There's a [3]c _ _ _ _ _ _ _ _ concert on [4]___________________. (27.08) Do you want to go?
A: Yes, please! I love Beethoven.
B: And on [5]___________________ (31.10) there's a [6]j _ _ _ concert.
A: Tell Mum and Dad. They love that kind of music.

▢ / 6

Grammar

3 Complete the text with the correct form of *be going to* and the verbs in the box.

get up go invite ~~not play~~ not stay

This weekend, my brother, Stuart, [0]*isn't going to play* tennis. He and I [1]______________ early and tidy our rooms. My big sister, Ruby, [2]______________ her friends to watch a film on TV. My parents [3]______________ to the cinema in the evening. They [4]______________ at home. What about you?

▢ / 4

4 Complete the dialogues with the words in the box. There is one extra word.

~~are~~ are going I'm is to

A: [0]*Are* you going to watch the show on TV tonight?
B: No, [1]________ not. It's boring.

A: [2]________ your mum going [3]________ buy a cake for the party?
B: Yes, she is.

A: What [4]________ you and your family going to do next weekend?
B: I'm not sure.

▢ / 4

5 Complete the questions.

0 **A:** Who can *you see* in front of the theatre?
B: I can see my favourite actor!
1 **A:** Have __________ an invitation to the party?
B: Yes, I've got an invitation to the party. You?
2 **A:** When does ____________________?
B: The football match starts at six o'clock.
3 **A:** Why are ____________________?
B: They're running because they're late for school.
4 **A:** Where did ______________ last summer?
B: Joshua went to England last summer.
5 **A:** How many new friends did ______________ on holiday?
B: I made five new friends on holiday!

▢ / 5

Communication

6 Complete the dialogue with the words in the box. There is one extra word.

~~busy~~ do let's meet sounds tickets would

A: Are you [0]*busy* next Saturday?
B: No, I'm not.
A: I've got [1]________ for a pop concert. [2]________ you like to come?
B: Thanks. That [3]________ great.
A: What time is it?
B: It starts at eight. Where shall we [4]________?
A: [5]________ meet at my house. We can go there together.
B: Great. See you then.

▢ / 5

Vocabulary	▢ / 12	Communication	▢ / 5
Grammar	▢ / 13	**Your total score**	▢ / 30

Language Test B

name ______________________ class ________

Vocabulary

1 Write the names of events.

0 We celebrate a special day.
a b_irthda_**y party**

1 We cook sausages and meat in the garden.
a b__________**e**

2 We go to the park or the beach and take food and drink with us. **a p**__________**c**

3 We watch actors in the theatre. **a p**__________**y**

4 We sing, dance or act in front of other people and the best person wins.
a talent c__________**n**

5 We wear costumes and have a lot of fun.
a f________**y d**__________**s party**

6 We go to a friend's house and sleep there.
a s__________**r**

☐ / [6]

2 Write the types of music and dates.

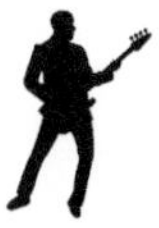

A: There are great concerts in our town this year.

B: Cool! I'd love to go to the [0]**r** _o c k_ concert. When is it?

A: It's on [0]_the third of April_. (3.04)

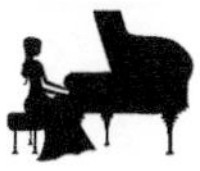

B: When is the [1]**c**_ _ _ _ _ _ _ _ concert? I'd love to go.

A: It's on [2]__________________. (19.06)

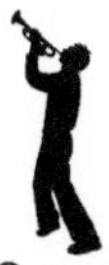

B: And look! On [3]__________________ (13.09) there's a [4]**j**_ _ _ concert. Do you want to go?

A: No, thanks! I don't like that kind of music.

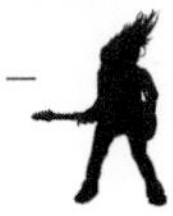

B: I love it. And I want to go to the [5]**r**_ _ _ _ _ concert on [6]__________________. (22.11)

A: Me too.

☐ / [6]

Grammar

3 Complete the text with the correct form of *be going to* and the verbs in the box.

buy do not go invite ~~not play~~

Next weekend, my sister Evelyn [0]_isn't going to play_ tennis. She and I [1]__________________ some jobs around the house. My big brother Gilbert [2]__________________ a new motorbike! Exciting! My mum and dad [3]__________________ their friends for dinner. They [4]__________________ to the cinema. What about you?

☐ / [4]

4 Complete the dialogues with the words in the box. There is one extra word.

am ~~are~~ are going is to

A: [0]_Are_ you going to watch the dance show on TV tonight?

B: Yes, I [1]__________. I love that programme!

A: Where [2]__________ your grandparents going to go this summer?

B: I'm not sure.

A: [3]__________ Mrs Lewis [4]__________ to teach us History next year?

B: No, she isn't.

☐ / [4]

5 Complete the questions.

0 **A:** Who can _you see_ in front of the theatre?
B: I can see my favourite actor!

1 **A:** How does __________________ to school?
B: Jasper goes to school by bus.

2 **A:** How many computer games have __________?
B: We've got six computer games.

3 **A:** What did __________________ yesterday?
B: Melissa made a chocolate cake yesterday.

4 **A:** Where are __________________?
B: The children are playing on the beach.

5 **A:** Why did __________________ to bed early?
B: I went to bed early because I was tired.

☐ / [5]

Communication

6 Complete the dialogue with the words in the box. There is one extra word.

~~busy~~ go I'd let's like shall sounds

A: Are you [0]_busy_ next Saturday?

B: No, I'm not.

A: I've got tickets for a football match. Would you [1]__________ to come with me?

B: That [2]__________ great. [3]__________ love to come!

A: What time is it?

B: It starts at half past five. Where [4]__________ we meet?

A: [5]__________ meet in front of the stadium.

B: See you on Saturday!

☐ / [5]

Vocabulary	☐ / [12]	Communication	☐ / [5]
Grammar	☐ / [13]	**Your total score**	☐ / [30]

name _____ class _____

Listening

1 🔊 2 Listen and match people 1–5 with places a–f. There is one extra place.

0 – g Brian

1 – ☐ Sybil

2 – ☐ Derek

3 – ☐ Mr Fisher

4 – ☐ Gloria

5 – ☐ Miss Anderson

 a

 b

 c

 d

 e

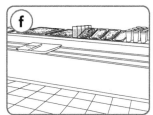 f

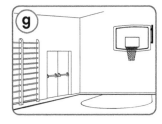 g

☐ / 5

2 🔊 3 Listen and complete the notes with food products. Write one word in each gap.

> **SATURDAY**
>
> **Breakfast:**
> orange juice,
> toast, butter and ⁰jam, ¹ _____
>
> **Lunch:**
> ² _____ with tomatoes and cheese
> ³ _____
>
> **Dinner:**
> chicken and a ⁴ _____
> ⁵ _____ with strawberries

☐ / 5

Communication

3 Read and circle the correct answer.

0 A: Hi, Dolly. I want to send you some photos. What's your email address?
  D: a D-O-L-O-R-E-S, S-A-N-C-H-E-Z.
     b 26 Village Road.
     © dolorez.sanchez8@xyz.com.

1 A: What are those things in your school bag?
  D: a They're my ballet shoes.
     b It's my calculator.
     c My Geography book.

2 A: Do you have a Music lesson today?
  D: a Yes, I can.
     b No, I don't.
     c No, I haven't.

3 A: Would you like anything to eat?
  D: a Yes, I like.
     b No, I like eating.
     c I'd like a sandwich.

4 A: Anything else?
  D: a No, thanks.
     b Yes, there is.
     c No, we don't.

5 A: How many tests do you have this week?
  D: a They're good.
     b Two – Maths and English.
     c There are some tests.

☐ / 5

1&2 Skills Test A

name ____________________ class ________

Reading

4 Read the text and write *T* (true) or *F* (false).

HOME | ABOUT ME | CONTACT

A day in the life of a ballet student

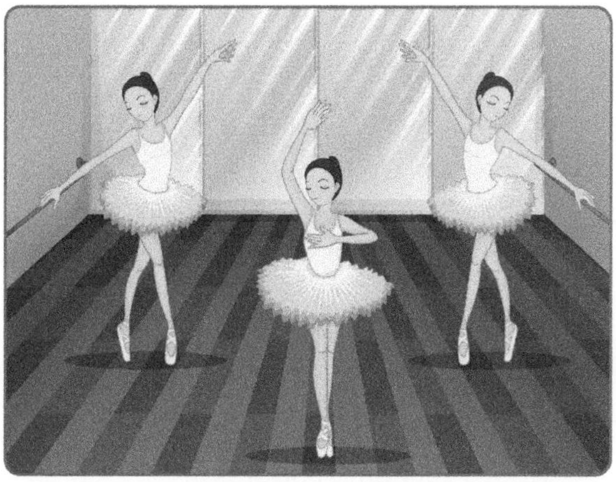

Michelle is a student at the Blanchard School of Ballet. She has lessons six days a week. On school days she gets up at seven and has breakfast in the canteen. The students and teachers eat together. Michelle has eggs, bread, jam and a glass of milk. Lessons start at half past eight. Michelle studies Maths, Science, Geography, History, Music, English, French and Italian.

Michelle has one ballet class at twelve o'clock. Then she has lunch. She doesn't eat a lot of food because she does ballet after lunch too. She practises from two to five. Then the last lesson of the day is an acting class. After that Michelle has a shower and she does her homework. Dinner is at eight and bedtime is at nine.

On Sundays there aren't any lessons. Michelle writes emails, plays tennis and talks to her friends. She goes to bed early and the school week begins again.

0 There are lessons every day at the Blanchard School of Ballet. [F]
1 Michelle has breakfast with the other students at the school. ☐
2 Michelle studies eight subjects at school. ☐
3 Michelle has a big lunch on school days. ☐
4 Michelle studies acting in the afternoon. ☐
5 Michelle does her homework before she has a shower. ☐

☐ / [5]

5 Complete the text with the words in the box. There is one extra word.

~~a~~ any bar carton don't eggs sugar

Hi Ivor,

Do you want to make ice cream at home? I've got [0] _a_ great recipe for you and you [1] ________ need a lot of things. I'm sure there are [2] ________, a [3] ________ of cream, a [4] ________ of chocolate and some [5] ________ in your kitchen.

See you at the weekend. Jill

☐ / [5]

Writing

6 Write 60–70 words about a day in your life at school. Use the questions to help you.

- What time do you get up?
- What do you have for breakfast?
- What time do lessons begin?
- What are you favourite subjects?
- Where do you have lunch?
- When do lessons finish?

____
____
____
____
____
____

☐ / [5]

Listening	☐ / [10]	Communication	☐ / [5]
Reading	☐ / [10]	Writing	☐ / [5]
		Your total score	☐ / [30]

1&2 Skills Test B

name ______________________ class ________

Listening

1 🔊 **2 Listen and match people 1–5 with places a–f. There is one extra place.**

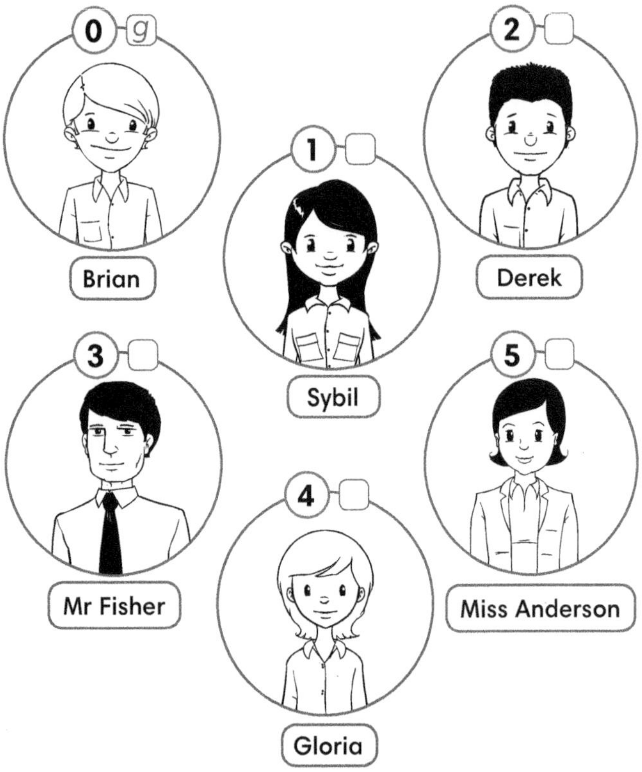
0 g
Brian
1
Sybil
2
Derek
3
Mr Fisher
4
Gloria
5
Miss Anderson

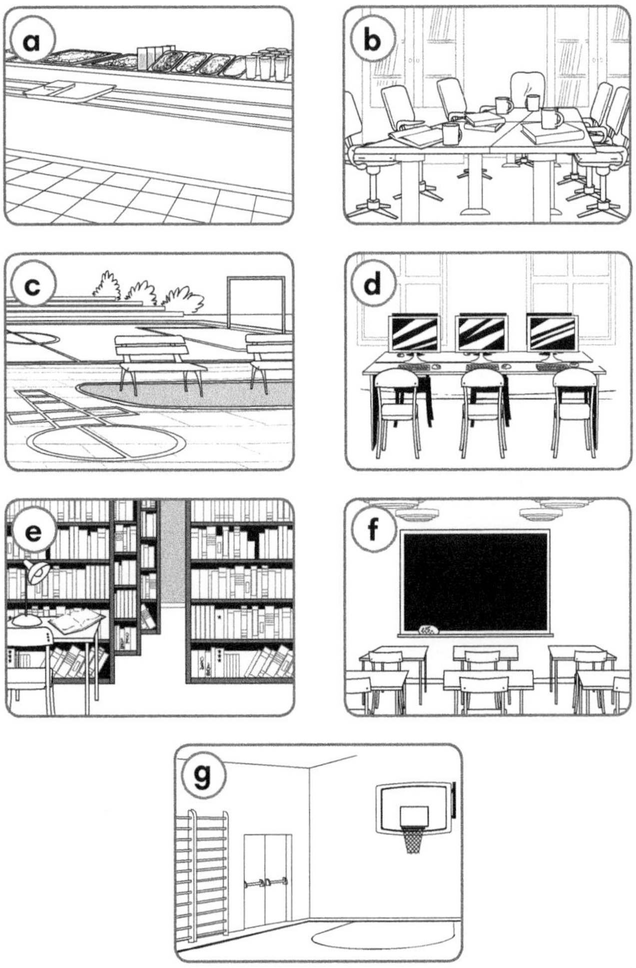
a
b
c
d
e
f
g

☐/5

2 🔊 **3 Listen and complete the notes with food products. Write one word in each gap.**

SATURDAY

Breakfast:

orange juice

toast, butter and [0] *jam*, [1] ____________

Lunch:

pasta with [2] ____________ and [3] ____________

fruit

Dinner:

[4] ____________ and a salad

pancakes with [5] ____________

☐/5

Communication

3 Read and circle the correct answer.

0 A: Hi, Dolly. I want to send you some photos. What's your email address?

D: a D-O-L-O-R-E-S, S-A-N-C-H-E-Z.

b 26 Village Road.

(c) dolorez.sanchez8@xyz.com.

1 A: Do you have a Science lesson today?

D: a Yes, I do.

b No, I haven't.

c Yes, I can.

2 A: Anything else?

D: a Yes, there is.

b No, thanks.

c Yes, we are.

3 A: What would you like to drink?

D: a Yes, please.

b Yes, I love it.

c I'd like a can of cola.

4 A: How many music lessons do you have this week?

D: a There are some tests.

b They're good.

c Two – one on Wednesday and one on Friday.

5 A: What's that thing in your school bag?

D: a They're my trainers.

b It's my calculator.

c My English books.

☐/5

name _______________ class _______________

Reading

4 Read the text and write *T* (true) or *F* (false).

HOME | ABOUT ME | CONTACT

A day in the life of a ballet student

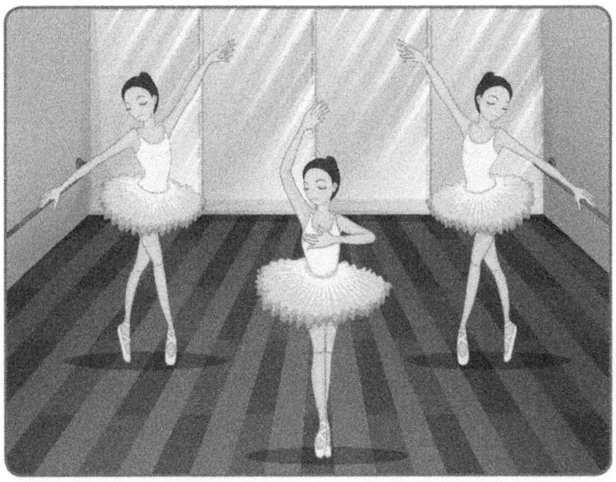

Louise is a student at the Aubert School of Ballet. She has lessons from Monday to Saturday. She gets up at seven and has breakfast in the canteen. The students and teachers eat together. Louise has bread, jam and orange juice. Lessons start at half past eight. Louise studies French, Science, Maths, History, Geography, Music, English and Italian.

Louise has ballet classes every afternoon. She has one class at twelve. Then she has lunch. She doesn't eat a lot of food because she does ballet after lunch too. She practises from two to five. Then the last lesson of the day is an acting class. After that Louise has a shower and she does her homework. Dinner is at eight and bedtime is at nine.

On Sundays there aren't any lessons. Louise talks to her friends and goes cycling. She goes to bed early and the school week begins again.

0 There are lessons every day at the Aubert School of Ballet. [F]
1 The teachers have breakfast with the students. [ ]
2 Louise studies seven subjects at school. [ ]
3 Louise never has lunch on school days. [ ]
4 Lessons finish at five o'clock. [ ]
5 Louise has a shower before she does her homework. [ ]

[ ] / [5]

5 Complete the text with the words in the box. There is one extra word.

are carton ~~do~~ eggs is lot sugar

Hi Ivor,

⁰*Do* you want to make ice cream at home? Here is a great recipe for you. You don't need a ¹__________ of things. I am sure you have got four ²__________ and a ³__________ of cream in your fridge. And I know there ⁴__________ a bar of chocolate and some ⁵__________ in your kitchen.

See you at the weekend. Jill

[ ] / [5]

Writing

6 Write 60–70 words about a day in your life at school. Use the questions to help you.

- What time do you get up?
- What do you have for breakfast?
- What time do lessons begin?
- What are you favourite subjects?
- Where do you have lunch?
- When do lessons finish?

____
____
____
____
____
____

[ ] / [5]

Listening	[ ] / [10]	Communication	[ ] / [5]
Reading	[ ] / [10]	Writing	[ ] / [5]
		Your total score	[ ] / [30]

3&4 Skills Test A

name ______________________ class ________

Listening

1 🔊 4 **Listen and draw lines. There is one extra name.**

Mum   Emily   Dennis   Lawrence

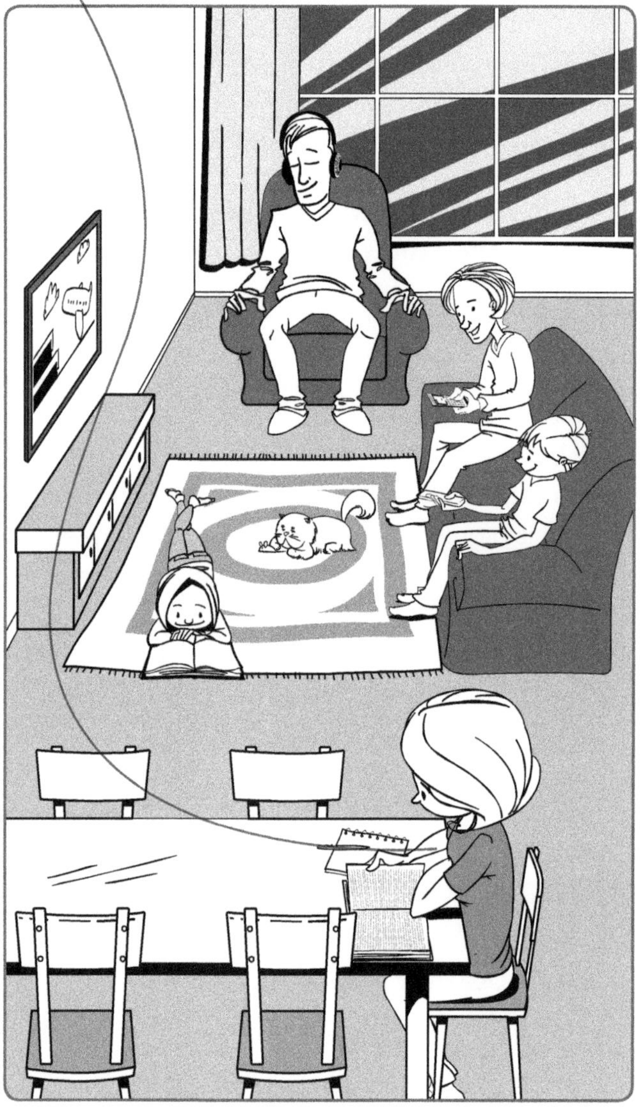

Dad   Muppet   Sabina

☐ / 5

2 🔊 5 **What places do they describe? Listen and match speakers 1–5 with places a–e.**

Speaker 0	*f*	a	the forest
Speaker 1	☐	b	the desert
Speaker 2	☐	c	the mountains
Speaker 3	☐	d	a big city
Speaker 4	☐	e	a small town
Speaker 5	☐	f	the beach

☐ / 5

Communication

3 **Look at pictures 1–5. Match them with sentences a–g. There are two extra sentences.**

0 *h*

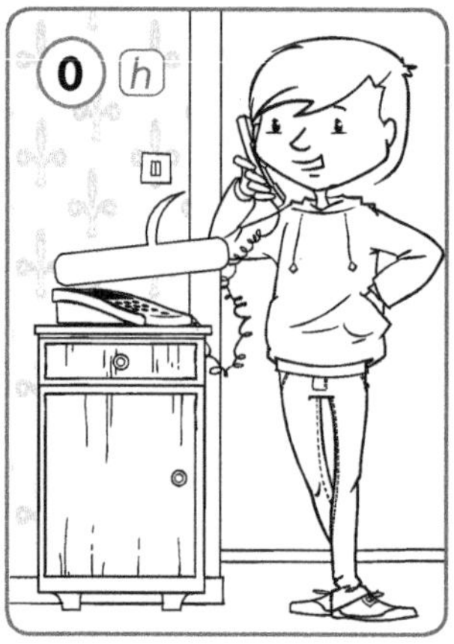

1 ☐

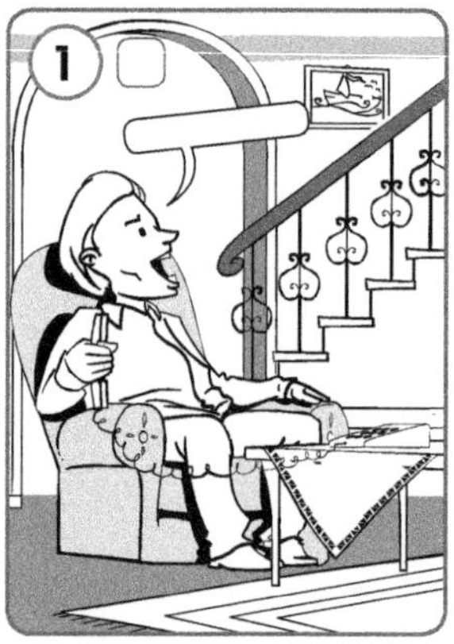

2 ☐

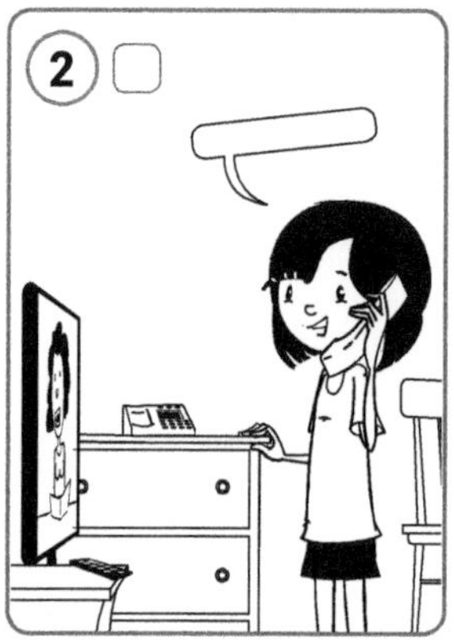

3 ☐

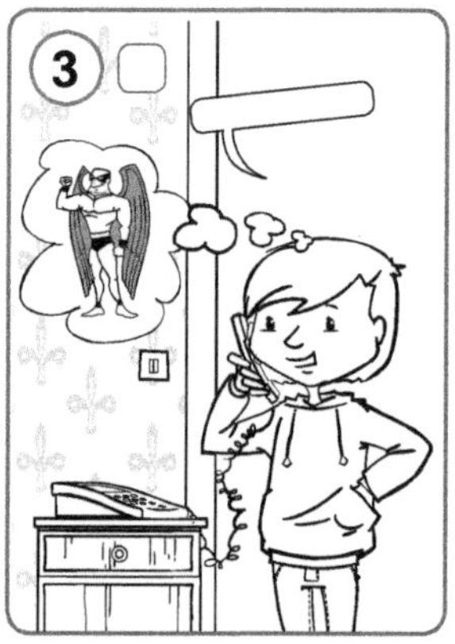

4 ☐

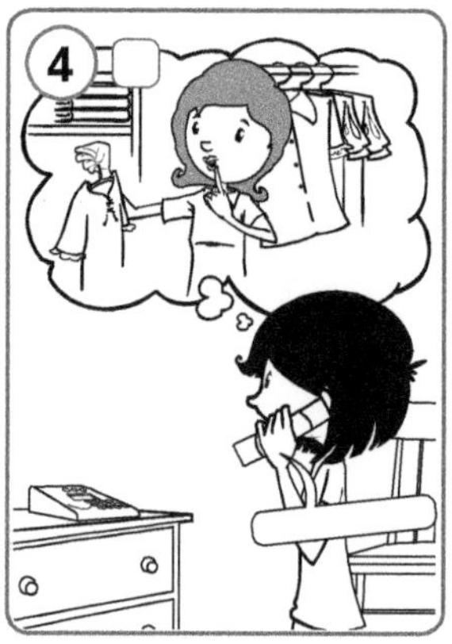

5

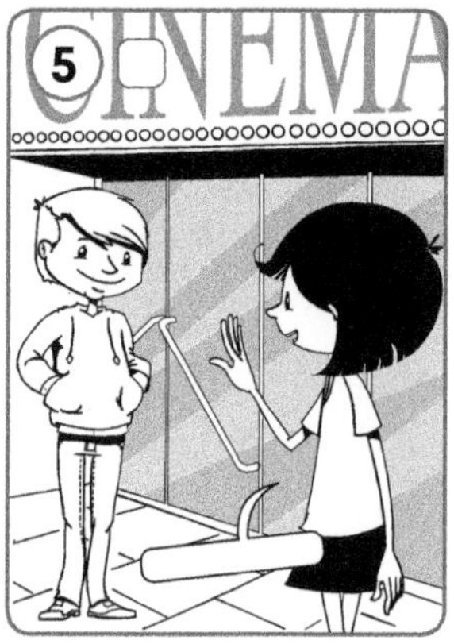

a Cartoons are a bit silly but we can watch Birdman II at the cinema.

b What about you?

c Bye. See you soon.

d No, I'm afraid Wanda's out.

e Just one moment, Fred. Kim! It's Fred for you!

f So what? I think it's boring.

g There's a cartoon on TV. Do you want to come and watch it with me?

h Hello, Mr Davies. It's Fred here. Can I speak to Kim, please?

☐ / 5

name ______________________ class ________

Reading

4 Read Penny's diary and answer the questions. Write full sentences.

23rd July

It's day number one of our holiday. We usually go to Spain in the summer. We love it there but this year we're in Corsica, in France. It's a beautiful island!

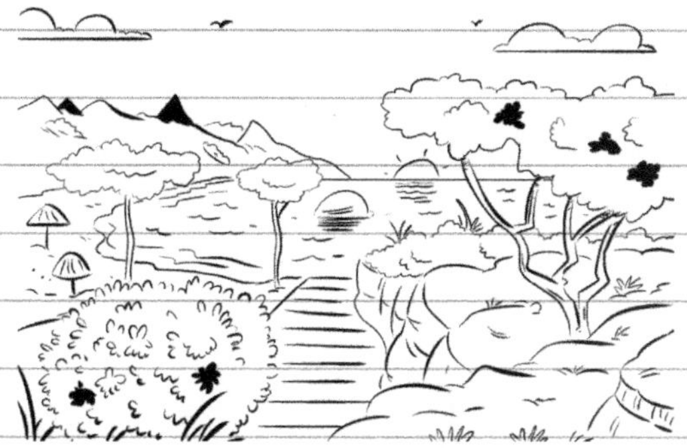

27th July

There are white beaches and you can go swimming, windsurfing and sailing. But today I'm swimming in a lake! There are a lot of lakes and rivers here. The longest river is the Golo – it's 90 kilometres long. I want to swim in the lake again but Mum says the sea is better. She doesn't like cold water and the water in the lake is cold!

1st August

It's a beautiful day. We're walking in the mountains. You can go mountain biking too. I want to go rock climbing but Dad says it's too dangerous.

3rd August

Today we're in Ajaccio. Ajaccio is next to the sea and it's the coolest town on the island. I love the shops here. It's lunch time now and we're sitting under an umbrella and eating sausages and cheese. Yum!

0 Where does Penny usually go on holiday?
She usually goes to Spain.

1 What water sports can you do in Corsica?
____

2 How long is the Golo river? ______________________

3 Why doesn't Penny's mum like swimming in the lake? ______________________

4 What does Penny's dad think about rock climbing? ______________________

5 It's 3rd August. What are Penny and her family eating? ______________________

___ / 5

5 Complete the text with the words in the box. There is one extra word.

~~bored~~ chat downloads interested scared selfies tablet

My brother and I love technology and when we can't use it, we're 0*bored*. My favourite technology is my 1_______. I take it everywhere with me. When I'm on holiday I use it to 2_______ online with my friends and take 3_______. My brother's favourite technology is his laptop. He's 4_______ in music and he 5_______ a lot of songs.

___ / 5

Writing

6 Write 60–70 words about your friend and compare him/her with you.

- What's your friend's name?
- Compare his/her and your appearance.
- What do you two like doing in your free time?
- What is he/she interested in? What about you?
- What is he/she good/bad at? What about you?
- Where does he/she like spending holidays?

____
____
____
____
____
____

___ / 5

Listening	___ / 10	Communication	___ / 5
Reading	___ / 10	Writing	___ / 5
		Your total score	___ / 30

3&4 Skills Test B

name ______________________ class ______

Listening

1 🔊 **4 Listen and draw lines. There is one extra name.**

[Mum] [Lawrence] [Sabina] [Dennis]

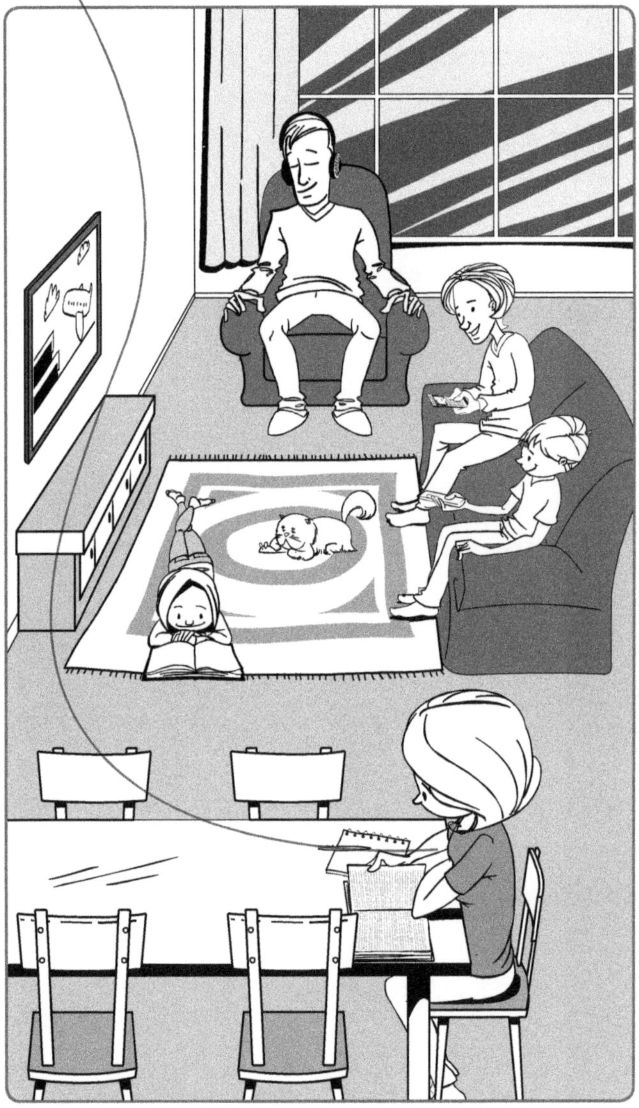

[Emily] [Muppet] [Dad]

☐ / 5

2 🔊 **5 What places do they describe? Listen and match speakers 1–5 with places a–e.**

Speaker 0	*f*	a	a big city
Speaker 1	☐	b	the forest
Speaker 2	☐	c	the mountains
Speaker 3	☐	d	a small town
Speaker 4	☐	e	the desert
Speaker 5	☐	f	the beach

☐ / 5

Communication

3 **Look at pictures 1–5. Match them with sentences a–g. There are two extra sentences.**

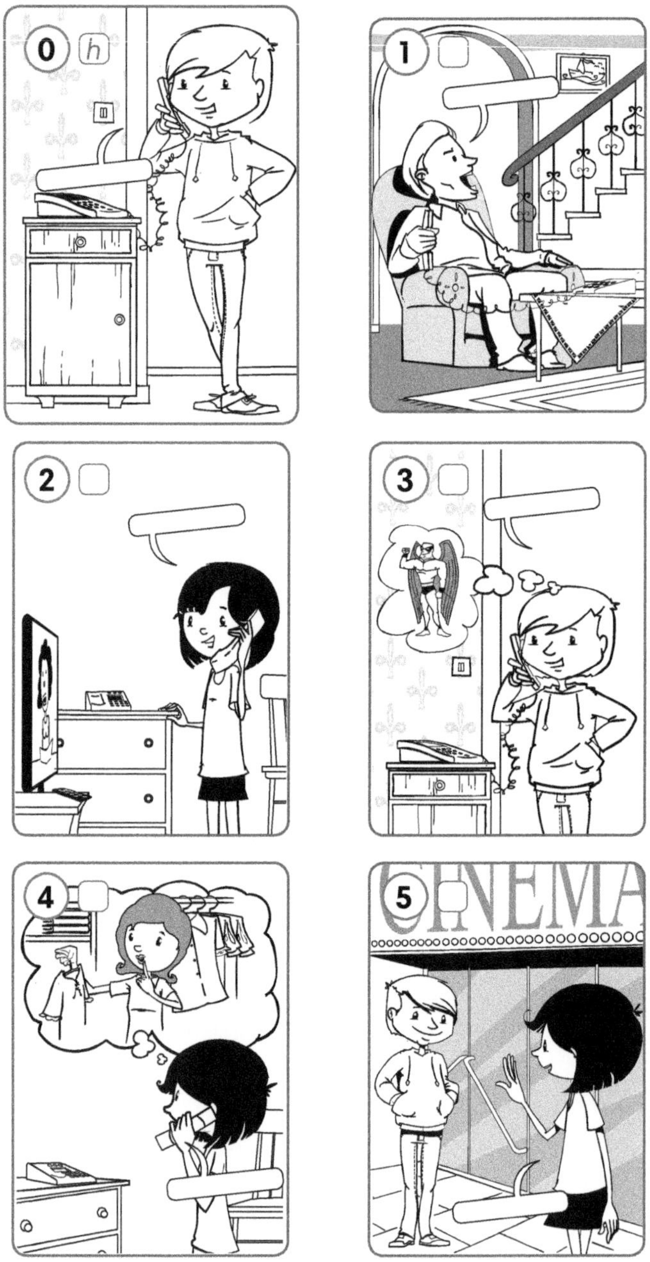

a Hang on, Damian. Alice! It's Damian for you!
b I'm afraid Gemma's out.
c In my opinion, cartoons are silly but we can go to the cinema and watch *Birdman II*.
d What about you?
e See you later.
f Why don't you come to my house and watch a cartoon with me?
g That's a surprise!
h Hi, Mr Marshall. It's Damian here. Can I speak to Alice, please?

☐ / 5

name ______ class ______

Reading

4 Read Joy's diary and answer the questions. Write full sentences.

23rd July
It's day number one of our holiday. We usually go to Spain in the summer. We love it there but this year we're in Corsica, in France. It's a beautiful island!

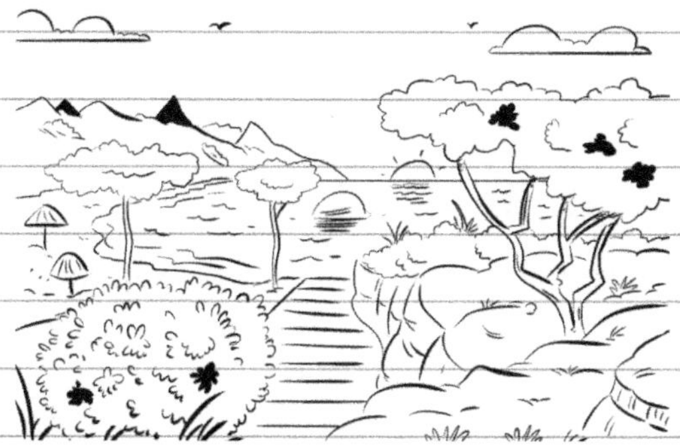

27th July
There are white beaches and you can go swimming, windsurfing and sailing. But today I'm swimming in a lake! There are a lot of lakes and rivers here. The longest river is the Golo – it's 90 kilometres long. I want to swim in the lake again but Mum says the sea is better. She doesn't like cold water and the water in the lake is cold!

1st August
It's a beautiful day. We're walking in the mountains. You can go mountain biking too. I want to go rock climbing but Dad says it's too dangerous.

3rd August
Today we're in Ajaccio. Ajaccio is next to the sea and it's the coolest town on the island. I love the shops here. It's lunch time now and we're sitting under an umbrella and eating sausages and cheese. Yum!

0 Where does Joy usually go on holiday?
She usually goes to Spain.

1 It's 27th July. Where is Joy swimming? ______

2 What does Joy's mum say about swimming in the lake? ______

3 What activities can you do in the mountains?
______

4 Where is Ajaccio? ______

5 It's 3rd August. Where are Joy and her family sitting? ______

☐ / 5

5 Complete the text with the words in the box. There is one extra word.

~~bored~~	chat	downloads	interested	scared
selfies	tablet			

My brother and I love technology and when we can't use it, we're [0]*bored*. My favourite technology is my [1]______. I take it everywhere with me. When I'm on holiday I use it to [2]______ online with my friends and take [3]______. My brother's favourite technology is his laptop. He's [4]______ in music and he [5]______ a lot of songs.

☐ / 5

Writing

6 Write 60–70 words about your friend and compare him/her with you.

- What's your friend's name?
- Compare his/her and your appearance.
- What do you two like doing in your free time?
- What is he/she interested in? What about you?
- What is he/she good/bad at? What about you?
- Where does he/she like spending holidays?

______
______
______
______
______
______

☐ / 5

Listening	☐ / 10	Communication	☐ / 5
Reading	☐ / 10	Writing	☐ / 5
		Your total score	☐ / 30

name _____   class _____

Listening

1 🔊 6 **Listen and tick the correct answer.**

0 Where was Charles yesterday afternoon?

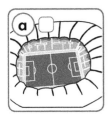 a ☐  b ☐  c ✓

1 What was the weather like in the morning?

 a ☐  b ☐  c ☐

2 What time was the film?

 a ☐  b ☐  c ☐

3 Where is the café?

 a ☐  b ☐  c ☐

4 What is Charles doing today?

 a ☐  b ☐  c ☐

5 What is Emma doing today?

 a ☐  b ☐  c ☐

☐ / 5

2 🔊 7 **Listen and answer the questions. Write one word or a number.**

0 Children often went to work when they were 15 or _16_.

1 Girls washed the floor and they washed the _____.

2 Girls looked after the _____ children in the family.

3 Boys often worked in the _____ garden.

4 Boys _____ their fathers fix things.

5 Farmers' sons looked after the _____.

☐ / 5

Communication

3 **Read the dialogue. Put the words in the correct order to make questions. Then write the questions in the dialogue.**

0 you / us / help / can ?

1 the / where's / Science Museum / ?

2 far / it / from / here / is / ?

3 walk / there / we / can / ?

4 we / to / can / get / how / Dover Street / ?

5 I / please / your pen / borrow / can / ?

Maggie:	Excuse me. I'm looking for the Science Museum. ⁰*Can you help us?*
Mrs Jones:	I'm sorry. What did you say?
Maggie:	¹ _____
Mrs Jones:	It's in the town centre.
Maggie:	² _____
Mrs Jones:	Yes, it is. It's three kilometres from here, on Dover Street.
Maggie:	³ _____
Mrs Jones:	Yes, you can.
Maggie:	⁴ _____
Mrs Jones:	Go straight on and turn left. Then go past the cinema and turn right. Then …
Maggie:	The directions are difficult.
Mrs Jones:	I can draw a map for you. Oh! I haven't got a pen. Excuse me, ⁵ _____
Man:	Sure, no problem.
Mrs Jones:	Thank you.

☐ / 5

5&6 Skills Test A

name ______________________ class ________

Reading

4 Read the text and write *T* (true), *F* (false) or *DS* (doesn't say).

HOME | ABOUT ME | CONTACT

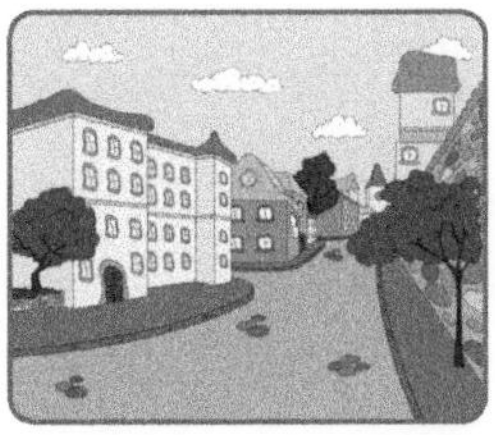

My town: past and present
by Dawn Cowper

In 1900 my town was very different. It was smaller and safer but it was also dirtier and more boring! In the centre of town, there were some shops, a bank and a library, but there weren't any hotels, museums or supermarkets. The nearest theatre was 56 kilometres away, and children played football in the street, not in a stadium. There were 13,000 people in the town and they lived in houses with small gardens.

Today the town is bigger. There are a lot of modern houses but you can see some older houses near the centre of town. There are also cafés, restaurants and an animal hospital. The town hasn't got a stadium but there's a sports centre.

My big sister doesn't live here now. She's a doctor and she works in a big city. I want to be a doctor too, but I want to be an animal doctor – a vet. I hope I can find a job at the animal hospital in my town when I finish school.

0 The town is bigger and more boring today. [*F*]
1 The town had a library in 1900. [ ]
2 There are 56 theatres in the town. [ ]
3 The houses in the past were small. [ ]
4 There aren't any modern houses in the centre of town. [ ]
5 Dawn's sister doesn't work in the town. [ ]

[ ] / 5

5 Complete the text with the words in the box. There is one extra word.

~~artist~~ chef looks nurse officer restaurant takes

Everyone in the Hamilton family works hard! Georgia is a(n) 0 *artist*. She's very talented and she draws great pictures. Her brother Cyril is talented too. He can sing and play the violin, but music is his hobby, not his job. Cyril is a 1 ___________ and he cooks fantastic food in a famous 2 ___________ in the city. Mrs Hamilton is a 3 ___________. She works in a big hospital and 4 ___________ after ill children. And Mr Hamilton, Georgia's father, is a police 5 ___________.

[ ] / 5

Writing

6 Write 60–70 words about a day out with your family or friends. Use the questions to help you.

- When and where did you go?
- Why did you go there?
- What did you do first?
- What did you do then?
- What did you do after that?
- How did you feel?

____

____

____

____

____

____

____

____

____

[ ] / 5

Listening	[ ] / 10	Communication	[ ] / 5
Reading	[ ] / 10	Writing	[ ] / 5
		Your total score	[ ] / 30

name ______________________ class ________

Listening

1 [6] Listen and tick the correct answer.

0 Where was Charles yesterday afternoon?

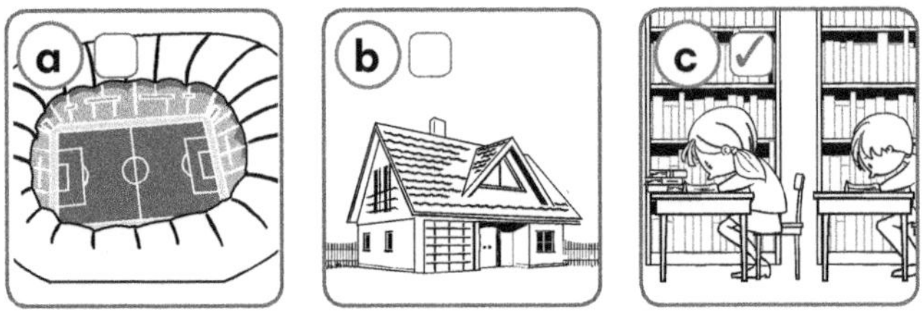

1 What was the weather like in the morning?

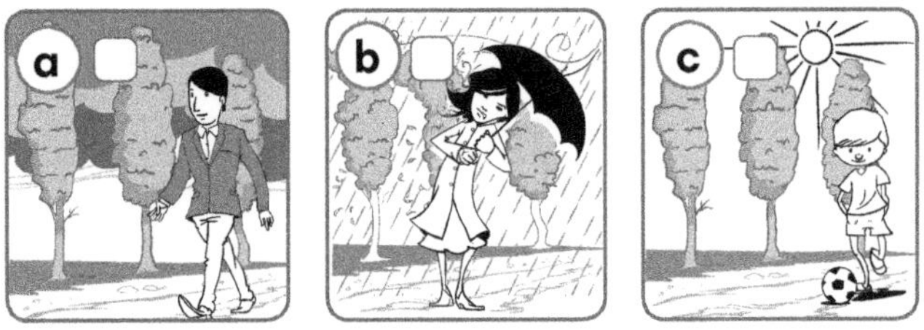

2 What time was the film?

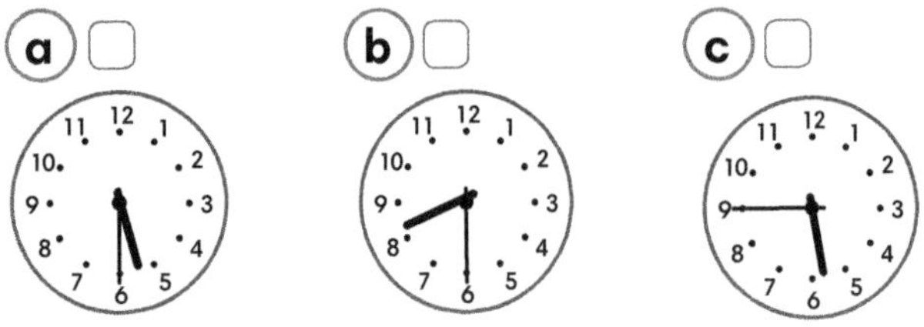

3 Where is the café?

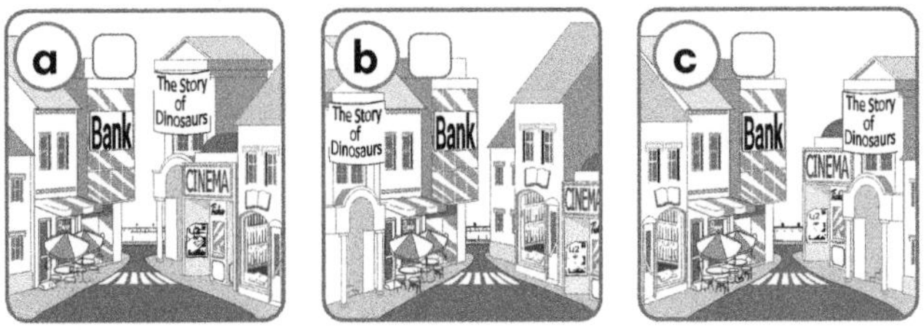

4 What is Charles doing today?

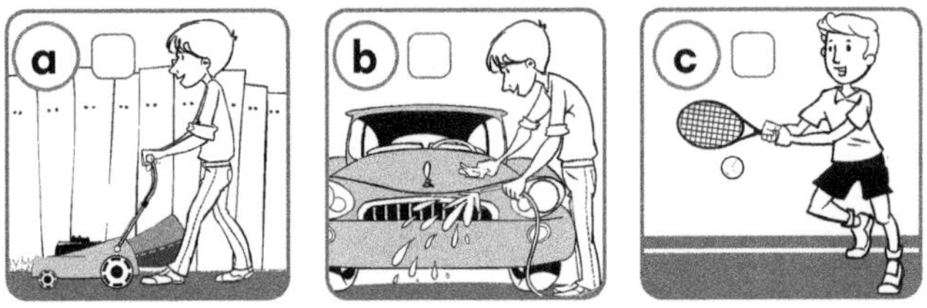

5 What is Emma doing today?

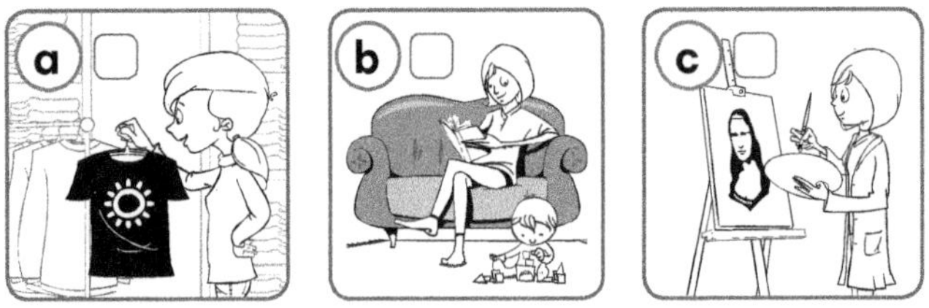

☐ / 5

2 [7] Listen and answer the questions. Write one word or a number.

0 Children often went to work when they were 15 or *16*.
1 Girls washed the ____________ and they washed the dishes too.
2 Girls looked after the younger ____________ in the family.
3 Boys often worked with their ____________.
4 Boys also helped ____________ things.
5 Farmers' sons also ____________ after the animals.

☐ / 5

Communication

3 Read the dialogue. Put the words in the correct order to make questions. Then write the questions in the dialogue.

0 you / us / help / can ?
1 History Museum / where's / the /?
2 from / it / far / is / here / ?
3 there / we / can / walk / ?
4 Suffolk Street / we / to / can / get / how / ?
5 I / your pen / please / borrow / can / ?

Daniel: Excuse me. I'm looking for the History Museum. [0]*Can you help us?*
Mrs Taylor: I'm sorry. What did you say?
Daniel: [1] ____________________
Mrs Taylor: It's in the city centre.
Daniel: [2] ____________________
Mrs Taylor: No, it isn't. It's two kilometres from here, on Suffolk Street.
Daniel: [3] ____________________
Mrs Taylor: Yes, you can.
Daniel: [4] ____________________
Mrs Taylor: Go straight on and turn right. Then go past the supermarket and turn left. Then …
Daniel: The directions are difficult.
Mrs Taylor: I can draw a map for you, but I haven't got a pen. Excuse me, [5] ____________________
Man: Sure, no problem. Here's a pen.
Daniel: Thank you.

☐ / 5

name _____   class _____

Reading

4 Read the text and write *T* (true), *F* (false) or *DS* (doesn't say).

HOME | ABOUT ME | CONTACT

My town: past and present
by Dawn Cowper

In 1900 my town was very different. It was smaller and safer but it was also dirtier and more boring! In the centre of town, there were some shops, a bank and a library, but there weren't any hotels, museums or supermarkets. The nearest theatre was 56 kilometres away, and children played football in the street, not in a stadium. There were 13,000 people in the town and they lived in houses with small gardens.

Today the town is bigger. There are a lot of modern houses but you can see some older houses near the centre of town. There are also cafés, restaurants and an animal hospital. The town hasn't got a stadium but there's a sports centre.

My big sister doesn't live here now. She's a doctor and she works in a big city. I want to be a doctor too, but I want to be an animal doctor – a vet. I hope I can find a job at the animal hospital in my town when I finish school.

0 The town is bigger and more boring today. [F]

1 The streets were very dirty in the past. ☐

2 In the past the town had a bank. ☐

3 There aren't any old houses in the centre of town now. ☐

4 There is a hospital for people in the town. ☐

5 Dawn's sister is a vet. ☐

☐ / 5

5 Complete the text with the words in the box. There is one extra word.

~~artist~~ assistant hospital looks nurse police takes

Everyone in the Morgan family works hard! Megan is a(n) ⁰*artist*. She's very talented and she draws great pictures. Her brother Llewellyn is talented too. He can play the piano and sing, but music is his hobby, not his job. Llewellyn is a shop ¹_____ and works in a clothes shop. Mrs Morgan works in a big ²_____. She isn't a doctor but she ³_____ after ill children. She's a ⁴_____ . Mr Morgan, Megan's father, is a ⁵_____ officer.

☐ / 5

Writing

6 Write 60–70 words about a day out with your family or friends. Use the questions to help you.

- When and where did you go?
- Why did you go there?
- What did you do first?
- What did you do then?
- What did you do after that?
- How did you feel?

_____
_____
_____
_____
_____
_____
_____
_____
_____
_____

☐ / 5

Listening	☐ / 10	Communication	☐ / 5
Reading	☐ / 10	Writing	☐ / 5
		Your total score	☐ / 30

name _____ class _____

Listening

1 🔊 **8 Listen to part of a radio programme. Is the information correct? Write yes or no.**

Events this summer

0	Football match – 14th June	_yes_
1	Talent show – 21st June, Royal Theatre	_____
2	Classical music 🙂 – 2nd July, Concert hall	_____
3	Jazz! Georgia Franklin 🙂🙂 – 13th July, Grantly Park	_____
4	Pop concert, (Three Ways) – 11th August, Grantly Park (*Tell Mark about this!*)	_____
5	Rock concert – 23rd August, Royal Theatre	_____

☐ / 5

2 🔊 **9 Edith is talking to Neil. Listen and answer the questions. Write short answers.**

0 Why is Neil's teacher angry?
Because Neil was late for school.

1 How does Neil sometimes go to school?
_____

2 Is there a bus from Neil's house to the school?
_____

3 How did Edith go to school this morning?
_____

4 What do Edith's parents think of motorbikes?
_____

5 What is the best transport in the children's opinion?
_____

☐ / 5

Communication

3 Look at pictures 1–5. Match them with sentences a–g. There are two extra sentences.

0 ⓗ  **1** ☐

2  **3**

4  **5**

a Come on! We're late!

b That's a pity.

c That's seven pounds forty, please.

d I'd like two tickets to Bracknell, please.

e Are you busy next weekend?

f That sounds great. I'd love to come.

g Let's meet at the train station at six o'clock.

h I've got two tickets for the rock concert on Friday evening.

☐ / 5

name ______________________ class ________

Reading

4 Read the story. Complete the sentences about the text with one, two or three words.

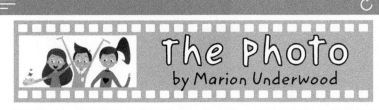

The Photo

by Marion Underwood

Last year I invited my Italian friend Elena to spend a week at my house. It was my thirteenth birthday that week and I wanted to see all my friends. Elena travelled to the UK by train and Mum and I met her at the train station.

0 Elena went to England last *year*.
0 Marion and her mum met Elena at the *train station*.

It was lunch time when we arrived home and we were hungry. Mum cooked a great meal and we ate a lot! After lunch, Elena wanted to go sightseeing so we went to town and she bought some souvenirs. Then we went to a café and had ice cream.

1 The girls were hungry because it was ____________.
2 Then they went ______________ in the town.

The next day, it was my birthday. 'I've got a present for you but it's a surprise,' said Elena. In the afternoon, we had a party next to the swimming pool and I wanted to take a photo of everyone with my mobile phone camera. There were a lot of people so I walked back … and back … The next minute I was in the swimming pool with all my clothes on – and my mobile phone!

3 Marion's birthday party was ______________ the swimming pool.
4 There were ______________ people at the party.

I got out of the water. 'Oh, no! My phone and camera don't work!' I said. 'Don't worry,' said Elena. 'This is your birthday present from me!'. It was a new camera! And this time I took some photos of all my friends – and I didn't fall into the pool again. It was a very special birthday!

5 Elena's present was a new ______________.

[ ] / 5

5 Complete the text with the words in the box. There is one extra word.

barbecue better drank take tents took ~~went~~

Yesterday my friends and I [0] *went* camping. We had our backpacks, [1] __________ and sleeping bags with us. We [2] __________ the bus and arrived at the camp in the afternoon. In the evening, we had a [3] __________ and we told funny jokes. We ate sausages and [4] __________ too much cola! It was [5] __________ than staying in an expensive hotel!

[ ] / 5

Writing

6 You are on holiday. Write a postcard of 60–70 words to your friend. Use the questions to help you.

- Where are you?
- Who is with you?
- Write about the weather.
- Where are you staying?
- What did you do yesterday?
- What are you going to do tomorrow?

Hi Alistair,

____
____
____
____
____
____
____
____
____

See you soon!
Neville

[ ] / 5

Listening	[ ] / 10	Communication	[ ] / 5
Reading	[ ] / 10	Writing	[ ] / 5
		Your total score	[ ] / 30

© Pearson Education Limited 2017 PHOTOCOPIABLE

name _____ class _____

Listening

1 🔊 **8 Listen to part of a radio programme. Is the information correct? Write yes or no.**

Events this summer

0 Football match – 14th June   _yes_

1 Dance show – 21st June, Royal Theatre   _____

2 Classical music 🙂 – 2nd July, Concert hall   _____

3 Jazz concert! Georgia Franklin 😊 😊 – 13th July, Grantly Park   _____

4 Pop concert (Three Ways) – 11th August, Grantly Park (*Tell Mark about this!*)   _____

5 Reggae concert – 3rd August, Royal Theatre   _____

☐ / 5

2 🔊 **9 Edith is talking to Neil. Listen and answer the questions. Write short answers.**

0 Why is Neil's teacher angry?
Because Neil was late for school.

1 Who sometimes drives Neil to school?

_____

2 Where does Edith live?

_____

3 Why didn't Neil come to school by bike?

_____

4 What has Neil's brother got?

_____

5 What does this town need?

_____

☐ / 5

Communication

3 Look at pictures 1–5. Match them with sentences a–g. There are two extra sentences.

a Let's meet at the train station at six o'clock.

b That sounds great. I'd love to come.

c I'd like two tickets to Bracknell, please.

d That's a pity.

e Come on! We're late!

f Are you busy next weekend?

g That's seven pounds forty, please.

h I've got two tickets for the rock concert on Friday evening.

☐ / 5

name _____ class _____

Reading

4 Read the story. Complete the sentences about the text with one, two or three words.

The Photo
by Marion Underwood

Last year I invited my Italian friend Elena to spend a week at my house. It was my thirteenth birthday that week and I wanted my friends with me. Elena travelled to the UK by train and Mum and I met her at the train station.

0 Elena went to England last *year*.
0 Marion and her mum met Elena at the *train station*.

It was lunch time when we arrived home and we were hungry. Mum cooked a great meal and we ate a lot! After lunch, Elena wanted to go sightseeing so we went to town and she bought some souvenirs. Then we went to a café and had ice cream.

1 It was lunch time so the girls were _____.
2 Elena wanted to go sightseeing so they went _____.

The next day, it was my birthday. 'I've got a present for you but it's a surprise,' said Elena. In the afternoon, we had a party next to the swimming pool and I wanted to take a photo of everyone with my mobile phone camera. There were a lot of people so I walked back … and back … The next minute I was in the swimming pool with all my clothes on – and my mobile phone!

3 Marion's birthday party was next to the _____.
4 There were a lot of _____ at the party.

I got out of the water. 'Oh, no! My phone and camera don't work!' I said. 'Don't worry,' said Elena. 'This is your birthday present from me!'. It was a new camera! And this time I took some photos of all my friends – and I didn't fall into the pool again. It was a very special birthday.

5 Marion _____ with her new camera.

☐ / 5

5 Complete the text with the words in the box. There is one extra word.

ate backpacks barbecue drank exciting took ~~went~~

Yesterday my friends and I ⁰*went* camping. We had our ¹_____, tents and sleeping bags with us. We ²_____ the bus and arrived at the camp in the afternoon. In the evening, we had a barbecue and we told funny jokes. We ³_____ sausages and ⁴_____ too much cola! It was more ⁵_____ than staying in an expensive hotel!

☐ / 5

Writing

6 You are on holiday. Write a postcard of 60–70 words to your friend. Use the questions to help you.

- Where are you?
- Who is with you?
- Write about the weather.
- Where are you staying?
- What did you do yesterday?
- What are you going to do tomorrow?

Hi Alistair,

_____
_____
_____
_____
_____
_____
_____
_____
_____

See you soon!
Neville

☐ / 5

Listening ☐ / 10	Communication ☐ / 5
Reading ☐ / 10	Writing ☐ / 5
	Your total score ☐ / 30

67

Mid-Year Test A

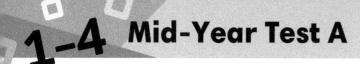

name ____________________ class ________

Vocabulary

1 Circle the odd one out.

0	Geography	Science	P.E.	(March)
1	calculator	coat	scissors	map
2	gym	canteen	shower	playground
3	carton	cereal	sugar	pasta
4	flour	can	jar	bottle
5	desert	volcano	city	river

[ ] / [5]

2 Circle the correct answer.

0 I am *drawing / riding / (cooking)* lunch in the kitchen.
1 Jake plays the *drums / basketball / tennis* in a band at the weekend.
2 The girls *play / make / do* ballet every Monday and Wednesday after school.
3 Dad is wearing his new *speakers / headphones / keyboards* and he is listening to music.
4 Young people don't usually buy CDs. They *take / download / text* songs from the Internet.
5 I'm very excited *about / in / at* our holiday!

[ ] / [5]

3 Complete the texts with the words in the box. There is one extra word.

angry ~~beautiful~~ expensive kind pretty scared tired

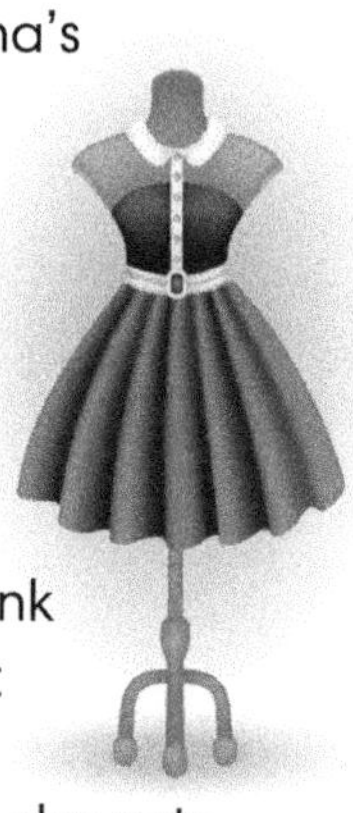

Ann: I want to buy this dress for Diana's party on Saturday.
Jess: It's 0*beautiful*! I love it!
Ann: Yes, but it's £49.99! That's too 1__________!
Jess: What about those dresses? They're cheap.
Ann: I don't like them. They've got pink rabbits on them but they aren't 2__________! They look silly. My sister's got a cool dress but she gets 3__________ when I take her clothes.
Jess: Ask your brother for money! He's 4__________ and he always helps you. Ask him now.
Ann: I can't. He's 5__________ and he's sleeping.
Jess: Ask him later.

[ ] / [5]

Grammar

4 Complete the text with the Present Simple form of the verbs.

> **My life** by *Geoff Craven*
> 2nd July
> My family and I 0*are always* (always / be) at home on Sunday evening. My brother 1__________ (not like) watching TV so he 2__________ (usually / listen) to music. My sister and I 3__________ (do) our homework. We 4__________ (not go) to bed late because we have school on Monday morning. How 5__________ (you / spend) your Sunday evenings?

[ ] / [5]

5 Complete the text with the Present Continuous form of the verbs in the box.

do not swim not wear run ~~sit~~ take

> **My life** by *Geoff Craven*
> 8th July
> Today I'm at the beach with my friends. I 0*am sitting* under an umbrella. We 1__________ because the water is too cold. Kevin and Sue 2__________ selfies. Jonathan 3__________ on the beach with Mr Smith, his dog. He 4__________ shoes! But what 5__________ (Mabel and Darren)? They've got some chocolate ice cream!

[ ] / [5]

6 Complete the sentences. Use one word in each gap.

0 There i*s* a lot of water in the river this summer.
1 Are there **a**__________ biscuits in the packet?
2 The elephant is big but the blue whale is **b**__________!
3 Rabbits are faster **t**__________ tortoises!
4 How **m**__________ butter do we need to make a cake?
5 I think Majorca is the **m**__________ beautiful island in the world.

[ ] / [5]

Vocabulary [ ] / [15]	Grammar [ ] / [15]
	Your total score [ ] / [30]

name   class

Listening

7 🔊 10 Listen and complete the notes. Write one word or number in each gap.

Brandon Murphy, actor

How old?   [0] 25 years old

Favourite sport: football, windsurfing

and [1] _____

Favourite food: fish and [2] _____

Doesn't like: [3] _____ and sausages

Hobbies: likes reading books

about History and

[4] _____

likes playing [5] _____

Favourite thing: his [6] _____ and phone

◯ / 6

Communication

8 Match questions 1-8 with answers a-i. There is one extra answer.

0 How do you spell your name?   `j`

1 What's your email address?   ◻

2 What would you like to drink?   ◻

3 Can I speak to Manuel, please?   ◻

4 What do you think of action films?   ◻

5 Anything else?   ◻

6 What's your favourite film?   ◻

7 I love pancakes. What about you?   ◻

8 Where do you live?   ◻

a A glass of water, please.

b No, thanks.

c bathshebaeverdene@fftmc.com

d In New York.

e See you later.

f In my opinion, they're great!

g *The Fellowship of the Ring.* I love it!

h I like them but cupcakes are nicer.

i Just a moment.

j B-A-T-H-S-H-E-B-A.

◯ / 8

Reading

9 Read the text and write *T* (true), *F* (false) or *DS* (doesn't say).

The van Buren family

Mr and Mrs van Buren travel a lot for their work and their children, Jackie and Miles, travel with them. The children have lessons every day, but not in a classroom. They learn at home, and 'home' is a different country every month.

This month the van Buren family are in Austria. Today, Jackie and Miles are visiting the Kunzhistorisches Museum in Vienna. Jackie is interested in history, so she is looking at some old things and writing an essay about Egyptian history. Miles is interested in art and he is studying some famous paintings.

The easiest subject for the children is Geography. They learn about it from real life: they visit a lot of countries and they see real rivers, lakes, islands, mountains and other geographical features. Mrs van Buren teaches them Maths and her husband teaches them Science. The children also use the Internet a lot. They send their homework to their parents' laptops and their parents talk about it with them.

They also chat with their friends in the UK.

0 Jackie and Miles don't have lessons.   `F`

1 The van Buren family are in Vienna today.   ◻

2 Jackie is writing about Egyptian paintings.   ◻

3 Miles doesn't like History.   ◻

4 Geography isn't a difficult subject for Jackie and Miles.   ◻

5 Mr van Buren teaches Jackie and Miles Maths and Science.   ◻

6 The children haven't got any friends in Austria.   ◻

◯ / 6

Listening ◯ / 6		Communication ◯ / 8	
Reading ◯ / 6		**Your total score** ◯ / 20	

Mid-Year Test B

name ____________________ class ______

Vocabulary

1 Circle the odd one out.

0	Geography	Science	P.E.	March
1	fridge	dictionary	scissors	ruler
2	hall	gym	playground	shirt
3	cereal	jar	sugar	jam
4	packet	can	butter	bottle
5	volcano	lake	town	forest

☐ / 5

2 Circle the correct answer.

0 I am *drawing / riding / cooking* lunch in the kitchen.

1 Kay plays *guitar / tennis / the drums* in a band on Mondays and Wednesdays.

2 The students *play / take / do* pottery. It's their hobby.

3 Mum has got new *speakers / printers / screens* because she loves listening to music.

4 I never buy CDs. I always *download / go / surf* songs from the Internet.

5 Rock climbing isn't a safe sport. It's *high / dangerous / strong.*

☐ / 5

3 Complete the texts with the words in the box. There is one extra word.

angry ~~boring~~ cheaper expensive pretty scared tired

Ann: I want to buy a dress for Donna's party but I don't like these dresses. They're [0]*boring*.

Jess: But that black dress is [1]__________!

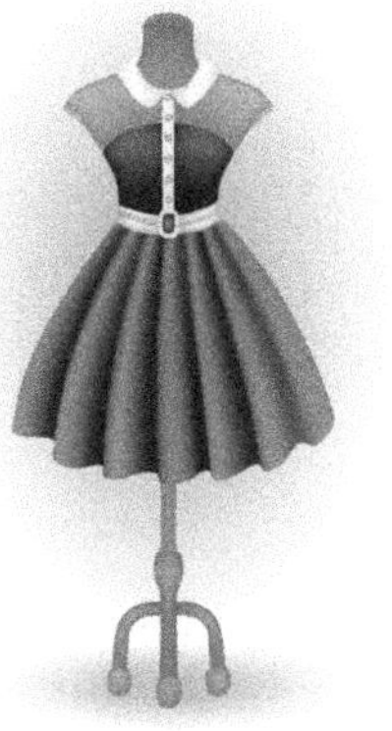

Ann: Yes, I love it! But it's £64.99! It's too [2]__________!

Jess: What about a top? Tops are [3]__________. You can buy a jumper for £15.

Ann: It's too warm for a jumper.

Jess: Go to another shop.

Ann: No, I'm [4]__________. I want to go home.

Jess: Your sister's got a cool dress. Why don't you wear that?

Ann: I can't. She gets [5]__________ when I take her clothes.

☐ / 5

Grammar

4 Complete the text with the Present Simple form of the verbs.

My life by Becky Taylor

2nd July

My family and I [0]*are always* (always / be) at home on Sunday evening. My sister [1]__________ (usually / play) computer games because she [2]__________ (not like) watching TV. My brother and I [3]__________ (do) our homework. We [4]__________ (not have) a big dinner. What [5]__________ (you / do) on Sunday evenings?

☐ / 5

5 Complete the text with the Present Continuous form of the verbs in the box.

go not look not swim read ~~sit~~ take

My life by Becky Taylor

8th July

Today I'm at the beach with my friends. I [0]*am sitting* under an umbrella. Ruby and George [1]__________ photos. Clara [2]__________ at the sea. She [3]__________ a magazine. We [4]__________ because the water is too cold. But where [5]__________ (Lacey and Joe)? To the ice cream shop!

☐ / 5

6 Complete the sentences. Use one word in each gap.

0 There i*s* a lot of water in the river this summer.

1 Blue whales are bigger **t**__________ elephants!

2 I think football is the **m**__________ exciting sport in the world.

3 Is there **a**__________ flour in the kitchen?

4 How **m**__________ eggs do we need to make a cake?

5 Strawberry ice cream is good but chocolate ice cream is **b**__________.

☐ / 5

Vocabulary ☐ / 15		Grammar	☐ / 15
		Your total score	☐ / 30

name _____ class _____

Listening

7 🔊 10 Listen and complete the notes. Write one word or number in each gap.

Brandon Murphy, actor

How old?   0 <u>25</u> years old

Favourite sport: football, 1 _____ and karate

Favourite food: 2 _____ and salad

Doesn't like: ham and 3 _____

Hobbies: likes reading books about 4 _____ and Science likes playing 5 _____

Favourite thing: his tablet and 6 _____

☐ / ⑥

Communication

8 Match questions 1–8 with answers a–i. There is one extra answer.

0 How do you spell your name? — ⃞ⱼ

1 What would you like to eat? — ☐

2 What do you think of action films? — ☐

3 Where does your cousin live? — ☐

4 What's your email address? — ☐

5 Can I speak to Hannah, please? — ☐

6 My favourite vegetables are potatoes. What about you? — ☐

7 What's your favourite film? — ☐

8 Anything else? — ☐

a Hang on.

b *Toy Story 2.*

c gabrieloak@fftmc.com

d See you soon.

e I like them but I think tomatoes are the best.

f In Canada.

g No, thanks.

h A ham and cheese sandwich, please.

i In my opinion, they're great!

j G-A-B-R-I-E-L.

☐ / ⑧

Reading

9 Read the text and write T (true), F (false) or DS (doesn't say).

The van Buren family

Mr and Mrs van Buren travel a lot for their work and their children, Jackie and Miles, travel with them. The children have lessons every day, but not in a classroom. They learn at home, and 'home' is a different country every month.

This month the van Buren family are in Austria. Today, Jackie and Miles are visiting the Kunzhistorisches Museum in Vienna. Jackie is interested in history, so she is looking at some old things and writing an essay about Egyptian history. Miles is interested in art and he is studying some famous paintings.

The easiest subject for the children is Geography. They learn about it from real life: they visit a lot of countries and they see real rivers, lakes, islands, mountains and other geographical features. Mrs van Buren teaches them Maths and her husband teaches them Science. The children also use the Internet a lot. They send their homework to their parents' laptops and their parents talk about it with them.

They also chat with their friends in the UK.

0 Jackie and Miles don't have lessons. — ⃞F

1 The family are in Austria this month. — ☐

2 Jackie is writing an essay about paintings. — ☐

3 Miles loves History. — ☐

4 Jackie and Miles think Geography is an easy subject. — ☐

5 The children's father teaches them Maths. — ☐

6 The children have got a lot of friends in Austria. — ☐

☐ / ⑥

Listening ☐ / ⑥		Communication ☐ / ⑧	
Reading ☐ / ⑥		**Your total score** ☐ / ⑳	

1-8 End-of-Year Test A

name ______________________ class ________

Vocabulary

1 Circle the odd one out.

0	China	Turkey	*(Italian)*	France
1	milk	biscuits	pancakes	rice
2	speakers	maps	headphones	screens
3	vet	doctor	nurse	builder
4	plane	tram	underground	torch
5	canteen	museum	playground	gym

☐ / 5

2 Circle the correct answer.

0 You need a *(tent)* / *souvenir* / *bin* and a sleeping bag when you go camping.
1 Dave *makes* / *has* / *does* the shopping at the supermarket every Saturday.
2 The train *takes* / *gets* / *leaves* the station at five to seven and arrives in London at twenty past ten.
3 She is going to be a police *worker* / *officer* / *assistant* when she finishes school.
4 Are you going to look *for* / *after* / *about* your little sister this evening?
5 I washed the *dirty* / *quiet* / *low* clothes yesterday so they're clean now.

☐ / 5

3 Complete the blog with the words in the box. There is one extra word.

~~beautiful~~ concerts desert easy spend surf visit

Life in Australia

by Bruce McIntyre

Hi! I'm Bruce and this blog is about my life on a sheep farm in Australia. Australians are friendly and Australia is a [0]*beautiful* country. My family and I live far from town, near the [1]________. It's hot here and there aren't any rivers or trees. We don't often eat in restaurants, [2]________ museums or go to [3]________. We use computers to chat with our friends online and to [4]________ the Internet. Life isn't [5]________ here. It's difficult but we love it.

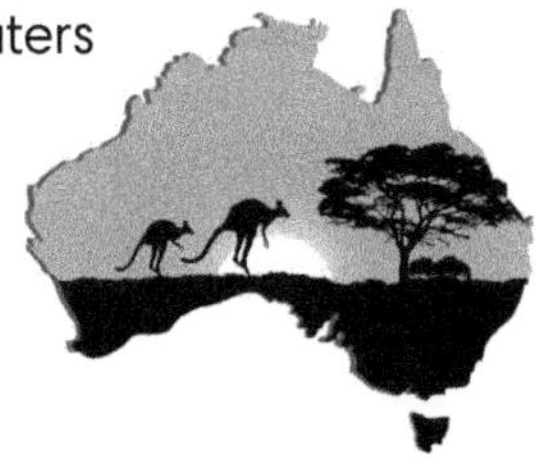

☐ / 5

Grammar

4 Circle the correct answer.

0 *(Those)* / *This* animals are very dangerous!
1 How *much* / *many* eggs are there in the fridge?
2 I think the pink flowers are *prettier* / *prettiest* than the white flowers.
3 Geraldine sent me an email *last* / *tomorrow* night.
4 In my opinion, 'Planet Earth II' is the *more* / *most* exciting programme on TV.
5 There weren't *some* / *any* cafés here in 2001.

☐ / 5

5 Complete the text with the correct form of the verbs in the box.

eat enjoy go ~~have~~ have not do

Hi Natalie!
I [0]*'m having* a lovely time at the moment in Spain. Mum and Dad [1]________ the holiday too. And Dad [2]________ swimming before breakfast every day! Yesterday morning we [3]________ a picnic in the mountains. It was fun. Then in the afternoon we [4]________ some typical Spanish food, *paella*, in a restaurant. Tomorrow we [5]________ anything exciting.
See you soon! Zoe

☐ / 5

6 Complete the questions.

V: Hi, Ellie. What [0]*are you doing*?
E: Hi Victor. I'm tidying my room. And Ricky is cooking pasta for lunch.
V: [1]______________________ lunch every day?
E: No, he doesn't cook lunch every day.
V: Where [2]______________________ yesterday?
E: I was at the football stadium yesterday. There was a football match.
V: [3]______________________ the match?
E: No, my team didn't win the match. The score was 1–0.
V: What [4]______________________ on TV last night?
E: I watched a programme about wild animals.
V: [5]______________________ for the English test tomorrow?
E: No, I'm not going to study for the English test tomorrow.

☐ / 5

Vocabulary ☐ / 15	Grammar ☐ / 15
	Your total score ☐ / 30

name _____   class _____

Listening

7 🔊 **11 Listen and answer the questions. Write short answers.**

0 What day did Maria call Jules? *last Friday*

1 What time did Maria call Jules? _____

2 What sport does Jules do every Friday? _____

3 How many hours was Jules at Bobby's house? _____

4 What was Jules worried about? _____

5 How did Jules go home from Bobby's house? _____

6 What date is the party? _____

☐ / ⑥

Communication

8 **Circle the correct answer.**

0 A: Would you like anything to drink?
   B: a No, I don't.
   ⓑ Yes, please.

1 A: Hello, it's Tom here. Can I speak to Cleo, please?
   B: a I'm afraid she's out.
   b You can speak.

2 A: What do you think of jazz?
   B: a I like listening to music.
   b In my opinion, it's the best music.

3 A: Excuse me, how can I get to the library?
   B: a You can get on the train.
   b Go straight on and turn left.

4 A: Can I borrow your calculator, please?
   B: a Sure, no problem.
   b Yes, I can.

5 A: I'd like a ticket to the zoo, please.
   B: a They're here.
   b It's six pounds, please.

6 A: What time does the bus leave?
   B: a At ten to six.
   b It's seven o'clock.

7 A: Are you busy next Friday afternoon? I've got tickets for a concert.
   B: a No, I can't.
   b That sounds great.

8 A: Where shall we meet?
   B: a Let's meet at eight o'clock.
   b Let's meet outside the bank.

☐ / ⑧

Reading

9 **Read the text and write T (true), F (false) or DS (doesn't say).**

My Family

by Lucilla Nucci

New York is an exciting city and people come here from all over the world. This is nothing new. In the past people came from Ireland, Germany, Sweden, Ukraine, Russia, Poland and a lot of other countries.

My grandfather's parents came to New York from Italy in 1923. Grandad's father, Giuseppe, didn't have any money and he didn't know any people in the USA. He was a builder and he worked very hard. At the weekend he painted people's houses. Grandad's mother, Francesca, didn't work but she looked after their children.

Roberto became a doctor. Cecilia was a fantastic singer and she also played the piano. Daniella had a restaurant and it was famous in New York. People loved her food. Antonio didn't like working indoors. He wanted to be a farmer so he left the city and went to California. He bought a farm there with fruit trees.

My mother and father work on the farm today. My sister and I love this place. But next month we are going to fly to New York. We still have family there and we are going to spend the summer with them.

0 People went to New York from six countries. ☐F☐

1 Lucilla's grandfather came to New York in 1923. ☐

2 Giuseppe and Francesca had four children. ☐

3 Roberto was Giuseppe and Francesca's oldest child. ☐

4 Daniella's restaurant was very good. ☐

5 Antonio's farm had orange trees. ☐

6 Lucilla and her sister live in New York. ☐

☐ / ⑥

Listening ☐ / ⑥	Communication ☐ / ⑧
Reading ☐ / ⑥	**Your total score** ☐ / ⑳

1–8 End-of-Year Test B

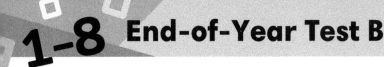

name ______________________ class ________

Vocabulary

1 Circle the odd one out.

0 China	Turkey	(Italian)	France
1 cereal	water	pasta	flour
2 scissors	printers	keyboards	screens
3 nurse	doctor	pilot	vet
4 rock	reggae	rap	tram
5 hall	hotel	gym	playground

☐ / 5

2 Circle the correct answer.

0 You need a (*tent*) / *souvenir* / *bin* and a sleeping bag when you go camping.

1 Mandy is a shop *officer* / *worker* / *assistant* in an expensive clothes shop.

2 I washed the dirty dishes this morning so they're *clean* / *low* / *quiet* now.

3 Kate always *has* / *makes* / *does* the beds in the morning.

4 The train *gets* / *leaves* / *takes* the station at half past and arrives here at nine.

5 I am going to look *in* / *about* / *after* my little brother this evening.

☐ / 5

3 Complete the blog with the words in the box. There is one extra word.

~~beautiful~~ difficult forest hotels online plays visit

Life in Australia

by Steve Loach

Hi! I'm Steve and this blog is about my life on a sheep farm in Australia. Australians are friendly and Australia is a [0] *beautiful* country. My family and I live far from town, near a [1] ________. There's a river near our farm and a lot of trees. We don't often eat in restaurants, go to see [2] ________ at the theatre or [3] ________ museums. We use computers to chat with our friends [4] ________ and to surf the Internet. Life isn't easy here. It's [5] ________ but we love it.

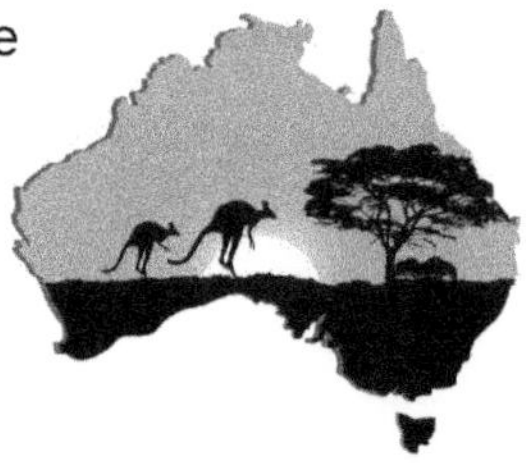

☐ / 5

Grammar

4 Circle the correct answer.

0 (*Those*) / *This* animals are very dangerous!

1 I think 'Planet Earth II' is the *more* / *most* interesting programme on TV.

2 Howard wrote a lot of emails *last* / *tomorrow* night.

3 There is *some* / *any* cheese in the fridge so we can make sandwiches.

4 How *much* / *many* milk is there in the kitchen?

5 Mount Everest is *higher* / *highest* than Mont Blanc.

☐ / 5

5 Complete the text with the correct form of the verbs in the box.

enjoy have go ~~have~~ meet not do

Hi Bruce!

I [0] *'m having* a fantastic time at the moment in Croatia. Mum and Dad [1] ________ the holiday too. And Mum [2] ________ running before breakfast every day! Yesterday we [3] ________ some friends in Dubrovnik. We went sightseeing and [4] ________ lots of fun together. Tomorrow we [5] ________ anything exciting.

See you soon! Harry

☐ / 5

6 Complete the questions.

A: Hi, Damian. What [0] *are you doing*?

D: Hi, Alicia. I'm tidying my room. And Priscilla is cooking pasta for dinner.

A: [1] ______________________ dinner every evening?

D: Yes, she cooks dinner every evening.

A: What [2] ______________________ on TV last night?

D: We watched a programme about wild animals.

A: Where [3] ______________________ last Saturday?

D: I was at the sports centre last Saturday. There was a basketball match.

A: [4] ______________________ the match?

D: No, my team didn't win the match. The score was 78–69.

A: [5] ______________________ for the Maths test tomorrow?

D: No, I'm not going to study for the Maths test tomorrow.

☐ / 5

Vocabulary	☐ / 15	Grammar	☐ / 15
		Your total score	☐ / 30

name _____ class _____

Listening

7 🔊 **11** Listen and answer the questions. Write short answers.

0 What day did Maria call Jules? *last Friday*

1 Where was Jules at three o'clock? _____

2 What time did Jules go to Bobby's house? _____

3 What was Jules worried about? _____

4 Who took Jules home? _____

5 What date is the party? _____

6 When is Jules going to write the invitations? _____

☐ / ⑥

Communication

8 Circle the correct answer.

0 A: Would you like anything to drink?
B: a No, I don't.
  (b) Yes, please.

1 A: Can I borrow your dictionary, please?
B: a Yes, I can.
  b Sure, no problem.

2 A: Where shall we meet?
B: a Let's meet at school.
  b Let's meet at half past seven.

3 A: What time does the train arrive?
B: a At five to five.
  b It's quarter to nine.

4 A: Hi, it's Peter here. Can I speak to Nadia, please?
B: a You can speak.
  b I'm afraid she's out.

5 A: Are you busy next Tuesday evening? I've got tickets for a concert.
B: a That sounds great.
  b No, I can't.

6 A: What do you think of classical music?
B: a I love listening.
  b In my opinion, it's the best music.

7 A: I'd like a ticket to the museum, please.
B: a It's two pounds fifty, please.
  b They're here.

8 A: Excuse me, how can I get to the museum?
B: a It's on the hotel.
  b Go straight on and turn right.

☐ / ⑧

Reading

9 Read the text and write *T* (true), *F* (false) or *DS* (doesn't say).

My Family
by Lucilla Nucci

New York is an exciting city and people come here from all over the world. This is nothing new. In the past people came from Ireland, Germany, Sweden, Ukraine, Russia, Poland and a lot of other countries.

My grandfather's parents came to New York from Italy in 1923. Grandad's father, Giuseppe, didn't have any money and he didn't know any people in the USA. He was a builder and he worked very hard. At the weekend he painted people's houses. Grandad's mother, Francesca, didn't work but she looked after their children.

Roberto became a doctor. Cecilia was a fantastic singer and she also played the piano. Daniella had a restaurant and it was famous in New York. People loved her food. Antonio didn't like working indoors. He wanted to be a farmer so he left the city and went to California. He bought a farm there with fruit trees.

My mother and father work on the farm today. My sister and I love this place. But next month we are going to fly to New York. We still have family there and we are going to spend the summer with them.

0 People went to New York from six countries. ☐ *F*

1 Lucilla's parents came to New York in 1923. ☐

2 Giuseppe was an artist. ☐

3 Cecilia was older than Daniella. ☐

4 Daniella had a good restaurant. ☐

5 There were apple trees on Antonio's farm. ☐

6 Lucilla and her sister want to visit New York. ☐

☐ / ⑥

| Listening ☐ / ⑥ | Communication ☐ / ⑧ |
| Reading ☐ / ⑥ | **Your total score** ☐ / ⑳ |

name _____ class _____

Part 1 Reading and Writing

Look and read. Choose the correct words and write them on the lines. There is one example.

a dictionary

a staff room

a bottle

potatoes

a mouse

a tablet

a desert

a volcano

Example

0 This is a small computer. *a tablet*

Questions

1 It doesn't often rain in this place and there aren't any trees. _____

2 These are big vegetables and you can make chips from them. _____

3 You use this book to find words and their meanings. _____

4 This mountain is very dangerous. _____

5 You can keep water, milk or orange juice in this. _____

6 This small thing helps you use a computer. _____

☐ / ⑥

name _____ class _____

Part 2 Reading and Writing

Read the text. Choose the right words and write them on the lines.

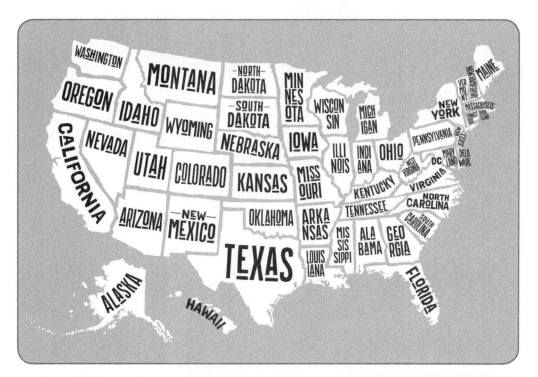

Texts: The Friendly State

What is ⁰*the* biggest state in the USA? A lot of people think it's Texas but that's not true. The answer is Alaska. Texas is number two and it's bigger
¹_____ California. People ²_____ that all men and women in Texas can ride horses, they're cowboys and they live in the country on farms
³_____ that's also wrong. Most people in Texas ⁴_____ live in the country. They live in big cities, like Houston, Dallas and Austin.

People from Texas love their state and think it's the best place in the world. They're friendly and they like ⁵_____ time with their friends at home. They cook outdoors and they eat ⁶_____ meat.

Example

0 a   some   (the)

Questions

1	as	from	than
2	think usually	often think	think always
3	and	but	because
4	don't	aren't	haven't
5	spend	spends	spending
6	a lot of	any	much

⬜ / ⑥

77

name _____ class _____

Part 3 Reading and Writing

Look, read and write.

LA BOUTIQUE
£1200

Examples

0 Two people are eating _pasta_.

0 What has the boy in the hoodie got in his hand? a _can of_ cola.

Complete the sentences.

1 The young man is listening to music with _____.

2 The man with the long hair is playing _____.

Answer the questions.

3 Where is the cat?

_____

4 What is the woman looking at?

_____

Now write two sentences about the picture.

5 _____

6 _____

☐ / ⑥

name _____ class _____

Part 4 Listening and Communication

🔊 12 Listen and draw lines. There is one example.

Steve

Molly

Anton

Clara

Ned

Jess

Oliver

Becky

☐ / 6

Part 5 Listening and Communication

Read the text and choose the best answer.

Example

0 Uncle Lee: Are you doing anything right now?
  Cilla: A Yes, I have.
           Ⓑ No, I'm not.
           C No, I don't.

Questions

1 Uncle Lee: Do you want to go to the cinema?
  Cilla: A Yes, good idea.
           B Yes, I know.
           C Yes, I am.

2 Uncle Lee: What do you think of action films?
  Cilla: A I'm thinking about them.
           B That's my opinion.
           C I think they're the best.

3 Uncle Lee: Would you like anything to eat first?
  Cilla: A Yes, please.
           B No, I don't.
           C Yes, I like something.

4 Uncle Lee: Anything else?
  Cilla: A No, I'm hungry.
           B I'd like some orange juice, please.
           C Yes, I'm eating a sandwich.

5 Uncle Lee: Where do you want to sit?
  Cilla: A Under the chair.
           B Behind the door.
           C Near the screen.

6 Uncle Lee: This film is exciting.
  Cilla: A I'm worried.
           B I agree.
           C I don't want it.

☐ / 6

Reading and Writing	☐ / 18
Listening and Communication	☐ / 12
Your total score	☐ / 30

name _____ class _____

Part 1 Reading and Writing

Read the story. Choose a word from the box. Write the correct word next to numbers 1–7. There is one example.

Jerome Adams was a ⁰*shop assistant*. He lived in Manchester but he
1_____ it. Manchester was a busy city and Jerome wanted to live
in a 2_____ place. He wasn't 3_____ in city life.

One day, Jerome's grandmother 4_____ him to her farm.
Jerome bought a train5_____ and travelled to the country.
His grandmother 6_____ him at the train station and they went to
the farm. 'I want to help you with the animals, Granny,' said Jerome.

He worked all day. In the evening Jerome was hungry and he 7_____
a big dinner. At nine he was tired so he went to bed. The next day, Jerome
said: 'I'm happy here. I'm going to be a farmer. Can I live with you, Granny?'
'Yes, you can!' said Granny.

Example

| shop assistant | banks | forests | interested | invited |

| met | quiet | ate | ticket | hated |

Now choose the best name for the story. Tick one box.

Jerome's new job ☐

Jerome's life in the city ☐

Jerome's exciting life ☐

___ / 8

name _____ class _____

Part 2 Reading and Writing

Look at the pictures and read the story. Write some words to complete the sentences about the story. You can use 1, 2 or 3 words.

A Holiday in Italy

Mr and Mrs Smith were interested in art and they wanted to go sightseeing in Italy. They bought new clothes for their holiday and they also bought guidebooks and maps. Mrs Smith was scared of flying so they didn't go to Italy by plane. They took the train and arrived in Rome on the second day of their holiday. They got off the train and took a taxi to their hotel. But when they went upstairs to their hotel room, they had a surprise. 'Where are the guidebooks and maps?' asked Mrs Smith. 'We didn't put them in the suitcase!' said Mr Smith. 'Now we can't go sightseeing.'

Examples

0 Mr and Mrs Smith wanted to go to Italy because they were interested in *art*.

0 They bought clothes, *guidebooks and maps* before their holiday.

Questions

1 They travelled by train because Mrs Smith was _____.
2 On the second day of their holiday they arrived in _____.
3 They went to their hotel by _____.
4 The guidebooks weren't in their _____.

Mr and Mrs Smith walked to the city centre. It was a beautiful day and the people were friendly. They met some nice Italians and they had coffee together in a café. They met their new friends again the next day … and the next. They didn't go sightseeing but they had a lot of fun.

5 Mr and Mrs Smith _____ with some nice Italians.
6 They _____ but they didn't go sightseeing.

Mr and Mrs Smith are going to go back to Italy next year. 'This time we are going to visit the museums,' says Mrs Smith. 'But now we have friends in Italy so we aren't going to bring our guidebooks with us.'

7 Next year Mr and Mrs want to go _____.
8 They are planning to visit _____ this time.

☐ / ⑧

name _____ class _____

Part 3 Listening and Communication

🔊 **13** Listen and write. There is one example.

A Day Out

Example

0 Place   Natural History *Museum*

Questions

1 Where is it?   Opposite _____

2 Date of visit   _____

3 Transport   by _____

4 Cost   _____ pounds

5 Museum shop   books and _____

6 Back at school   at _____

7 Afternoon   _____ about dinosaurs

☐ / ⑦

name _____   class _____

Part 4 Listening and Communication

Larry and Sylvia are school friends. They're talking about last summer. What are Larry's questions?
Write them in the spaces. The first one is an example.

Example

0 Larry: What *did you do last summer*?

0 Sylvia: I went to Australia with my family last summer.

Questions

1 Larry: Did _____?

  Sylvia: Yes, we had a fantastic time, thanks.

2 Larry: When _____?

  Sylvia: We went there in July.

3 Larry: Where _____?

  Sylvia: We stayed in Sydney, at my aunt's house.

4 Larry: Was _____?

  Sylvia: No, it wasn't hot. It was cool. July is winter in Australia.

5 Larry: Did _____?

  Sylvia: Yes, I did. I bought some cool souvenirs.

6 Larry: How many _____?

  Sylvia: I took hundreds of photos!

7 Larry: Are _____?

  Sylvia: No, we aren't going to go there again next year. It's far and the tickets are expensive!

☐ / ⑦

Reading and Writing	☐ / ⑯
Listening and Communication	☐ / ⑭
Your total score	☐ / ㉚

1&2 Speaking Tasks

Notes for the teacher

- **Vocabulary:** school subjects, school items, phrases with *do* and *play*, places in a school, food and drink, containers,
- **Grammar:** utterances using the Present Simple, adverbs of frequency, countable and uncountable nouns with *some* and *any*.

Task 1: Ask the student to look at the picture. Then ask the questions.

- This is Penny. What school items does she take to school?
- What subjects has Penny got today?
- What food and drink is there on the table?
- Is there (a can of cola) in the picture?
- Are there any (biscuits) in the picture?
- Why has Penny got ballet shoes? [To elicit: *Because she does ballet.*]

Task 2: Ask the student to talk about himself/ herself. Use these questions to help.

- What school items do you take to school with you?
- What are your favourite school subjects?
- Where do you do P.E.?
- What sports do you play in your P.E. lessons?
- Do you play any instruments/the piano in your Music lessons?
- Where do the teachers sit together at your school?
- What do you usually have for breakfast/lunch/dinner?
- Do you have lunch in the canteen at school or at home?
- What's your favourite food?

Philippa,
18 years old

Terry,
14 years old

Mr Lawson,
40 years old

Mrs Lawson,
42 years old

3&4 Speaking Tasks

Notes for the teacher

- **Vocabulary:** technology; using technology; geographical features; adjectives; adjectives to describe feelings,
- **Grammar:** utterances using the Present Continuous, comparative and superlative adjectives.

Task 1: Ask the student to look at the picture. Then ask the questions.

- This is a picture of the Lawson family home. Tell me about the place. [To elicit geographical features and adjectives, e.g. *beautiful, expensive (house), high (mountains), dangerous (sea)*]
- What are the people on the beach doing?
- How do the people (on the beach/in the water) feel?
- What is Mr Lawson/Terry/Philippa/Mrs Lawson doing? What is he/she using?
- Compare the people on the balcony. [To elicit: *the oldest/ youngest, older/younger than*]

Task 2: Ask the student to talk about himself/ herself. Use these questions to help.

- Tell me about the geographical features in your country.
- What is the longest river in your country?
- What is the highest mountain in your country?
- Has your house got a balcony? Compare your balcony with the balcony in the picture.
- Compare the people in your family. Who is the oldest/ youngest/kindest/most intelligent/friendliest/strongest?

Grantly in 1900

Grantly today

5&6 Speaking Tasks

Notes for the teacher

- **Vocabulary:** places in a town; prepositions of place; adjectives; jobs; jobs at home,
- **Grammar:** utterances using the Past Simple of *be; there was / were;* the Past Simple of regular and irregular verbs.

Task 1: Ask the student to look at the picture. Then ask the questions.

- These are pictures of the same town. This is the town in the year 1900. That is a picture of the town now.
- Tell me about the town in 1900. What buildings were there? Was it boring or interesting/quiet or busy etc.?
- Look at the two pictures. What is different?
- Where is the (theatre)?
- What's this man's/woman's job?
- Do you like this job? Why? Why not?
- How can I get from here to the bank/theatre/restaurant/ shop?

Task 2: Ask the student to talk about himself/ herself. Use these questions to help.

- Tell me about your town now. What buildings are there in your street?
- Is there (a stadium) in your town?
- Are there (a lot of restaurants) in your town?
- Is your street/town quieter/busier on Sundays or on Thursdays?
- Do you like your town? Why?
- How can I get from here to the nearest shop?
- What job do you want to do when you finish school?
- What jobs do you do at home?

&8 Speaking Tasks

Notes for the teacher

- **Vocabulary:** things to do on holiday; ordinal numbers (dates); types of music; events; travel equipment; transport verbs,
- **Grammar:** utterances using the Past Simple, *be going to*.

Task 1: Ask the student to look at the picture. Then ask the questions.

- Mr and Mrs Brown and their children went to France on holiday last year. This is a picture from their holiday.
- What do you think the Brown family did on holiday?
- What things did people take with them on holiday?
- When was the classical concert?
- When was the reggae concert?
- Where is the man with a suitcase from? [the UK/Great Britain] How did he travel to France?

Task 2: Ask the student to talk about himself/ herself. Use these questions to help.

- Did you go on holiday last year?
- Where did you go?
- What did you do there?
- How did you go there?
- What things did you (and your family) take with you?
- Do you like travelling by (train)?
- When is your birthday?
- What kind of music do you like?
- Where are you going to go on holiday next year?
- What are you going to do this weekend?

Unit 1 Classmates

Write 60–70 words about your school.
Use questions 1–5 to help you.

1 What time do lessons start at your school and what time do they finish?
2 What subjects do you study?
3 What is your favourite subject and why?
4 What activities do you do in the afternoon?
5 What time do you go home and what do you usually do in the evening?

Unit 2 Fun with food

Write 60–70 words about the food you eat.
Use questions 1–5 to help you.

1 What do you like having for breakfast?
2 Where do you have lunch and what do you eat and drink?
3 What do you like having for dinner?
4 What do you eat at the weekend?
5 What food don't you like?

Unit 3 Technology for all

Write 60–70 words about the technology you use every day. Use questions 1–5 to help you.

1 What is your favourite item of technology?
2 What do you do with it?
3 What other items of technology do you use a lot?
4 What do you do with them?
5 What do your parents think of technology?

Unit 4 Big world

Write 60–70 words about two family members (e.g. mother and father, mother and uncle, granny and grandad, aunt and uncle) and compare them. Use questions 1–5 to help you.

1 Who are the people and how old are they?
2 Describe their appearance.
3 Describe their personality.
4 What do they like doing?
5 What don't they like doing?

Unit 5 Around town

Write 60–70 words about an interesting part of your town or city. Use questions 1–5 to help you.

1 Where do you live? What is the most interesting street in your city/town?
2 What buildings are there in the street?
3 Describe the street (long, modern etc.).
4 What was different in the street 50 or 100 years ago?
5 What do you like about the street?

Unit 6 Just the job

Write 60–70 words about one day on your last holiday. Use questions 1–6 to help you.

1 Where were you?
2 How did you travel there?
3 What was the weather like?
4 Who was with you?
5 What did you do?
6 How did you feel?

Unit 7 Going places

You are on holiday. Write 60–70 words in a postcard to a family member. Use questions 1–6 to help you.

1 Where are you? Are you having a good time?
2 What's the weather like?
3 Where are you staying?
4 What did you do yesterday?
5 What are you doing today?
6 What are you going to do tomorrow?

Unit 8 Having fun

Invite the students at your school to a picnic. Use questions 1–6 to help you.

1 What is the event?
2 What date and time is the picnic?
3 Where is the picnic going to be?
4 What can people bring with them?
5 What can people do at the picnic?
6 Ask for a reply.

Audio script

🔊 **2 Skills Test 1&2**
Exercise 1

A: Angus F: Fiona

A: Hi, Fiona. Where's Brian? Is he in a French lesson?
F: Brian? No, he's got P.E. He's in the gym.
A: Is Sybil in the gym too?
F: No, she's got a Maths lesson.
A: Is that in Classroom 5A?
F: No, … Classroom 6C. … I think Derek's got Maths too.
A: Derek? No, he's got a test on Friday, so he's in the library. Have *you* got any tests this week?
F: Yes, Computer Studies, and I want to ask Mr Fisher some questions before the test. He's in the computer room, but there are some teachers with him.
A: Where's Gloria today?
F: She's having lunch in the canteen.
A: I want to talk to Miss Anderson. I think she's in the staff room.
F: No, she isn't. She's in the playground.
A: How do you know?
F: Because it's two o'clock and she always watches the kids in the playground at two o'clock.
A: OK. Thanks. Well, see you.
F: Bye!

🔊 **3 Skills Test 1&2**
Exercise 2

W: woman

W: Right. Let's see. What can we have on Saturday? … There are some oranges … We can have orange juice for breakfast. And there's some bread, so we can make toast. There's some butter in the fridge and a jar of jam. … Oh yes, and we can have eggs too.
Now lunch. Jeremy and Gwen hate fish, but they love pasta. So, pasta with tomatoes and cheese. … And then we can have some fruit.
Dinner … Hmm. Not fish. … I know! Everyone loves chicken and I can buy some vegetables and make a salad. And we can have pancakes with strawberries too. Good. That's done!

🔊 **4 Skills Test 3&4**
Exercise 1

D: Duncan AJ: Aunt Jo

AJ: Hello, Duncan. This is Aunt Jo. What is everyone doing?
D: Hi, Aunt Jo. Bella's at the cinema, but the rest of the family are at home.
AJ: Is your mum there too?
D: Yes, she's studying.
AJ: Studying?!
D: Yes, she's learning Spanish.
AJ: Oh! And how's Dennis?
D: Fine. He's watching TV.
AJ: Is he watching sport with Dad?
D: No, Dennis is watching a film and Dad's listening to music.
AJ: How can he listen to music with the TV on?
D: He's got headphones so he can't hear the TV.
AJ: Oh. … And how's Lawrence?
D: Lawrence? He's OK. He's playing with his mobile phone. … He's texting a friend.
AJ: Is everyone in the family using technology?!

D: No, Aunt Jo! Sabina is reading one of the Harry Potter books.
AJ: Oh, I love those!
D: And Muppet is playing with her toy mouse.
AJ: Clever Muppet. Anyway, Duncan, love to everyone. Goodnight.
D: Goodnight, Aunt Jo.

🔊 **5 Skills Test 3&4**
Exercise 2

N: narrator G1: girl 1 B1: boy 1 G2: girl 2
B2: boy 2 G3: girl 3 B3: boy 3

N: Example
G1: It's the best place to be. You can go swimming in the summer when it's hot. And in the winter, when it's cold, you can sit on a rock and watch the sea.
N: One
B1: I just *hate* walking around museums and things like that. *This* is the best place for a holiday. In the winter you can go skiing and in the summer you can go climbing.
N: Two
G2: It's hot in the day – too hot – but it's cold at night. There aren't any rivers or trees so living here is difficult. And it's often boring.
N: Three
B2: It's *beautiful* … There are lots of trees so I like this place very much. Birds and butterflies live here but there are snakes and other dangerous animals too.
N: Four
G3: I think it's an exciting place. There are a lot of people, fantastic museums, expensive shops … And I like going to different places every day so I don't like *small* towns.
N: Five
B3: Twenty-five thousand people live here. There aren't many shops but there are some good schools, two nice parks and an interesting museum. It's *better* than a big city.

🔊 **6 Skills Test 5&6**
Exercise 1

C: Charles E: Emma

N: Example. Where was Charles yesterday afternoon?
E: Hi Charles, I phoned your house yesterday but you weren't at home. Where were you?
C: I usually play football at the stadium on Friday but I went to the library. I wanted to study for the test on Monday.
N: One. What was the weather like in the morning?
E: *I* wanted to play football in the afternoon, but it was rainy and windy.
C: It was windy and rainy here too, but it was nice in the morning. Warm and sunny. And today it's cloudy and grey.
E: English weather!
N: Two. What time was the film?
E: What about yesterday evening?
C: I finished studying at half past five. Then I met Harry at quarter to six and we had something to eat at a café. Harry wanted to see a film in the evening but it started at half past eight. That's too late for me.
N: Three. Where is the café?
E: Was the café nice?
C: Yes, it was.

E: Were you at the new café opposite the cinema? Or the café between the bank and the museum?
C: No, we were at the café next to the library.
N: Four. What is Charles doing today?
E: What are you doing today?
C: Well, Mum's playing tennis with her friend, my sister's washing the car and I'm helping Dad. He's working in the garden. What about you?
N: Five. What is Emma doing today?
E: *My* mum's working at the shop today and Dad's making lunch. I want to paint. It's my hobby, you know, but I can't. I'm looking after my baby brother.
C: What about the test on Monday?
E: I studied last week but I can help you later if you want.
C: Thanks, Emma! You're a good friend.

🔊 **7 Skills Test 5&6**
Exercise 2

W: woman

W: In the past, children went to work when they were fifteen or sixteen years old. And younger children helped their parents at work or in the house.
Girls did a lot of jobs in the house. They made the beds and tidied the rooms. They washed the floors and helped their mother with the cooking. After meals, they washed the dishes. And who looked after the younger children? Not the boys! That was the girls' job.
But boys did jobs in the house too. They often worked in the vegetable garden with their father and helped him fix things. Farmers' sons also helped their fathers look after the animals.
Today, young people stay at school until they are sixteen, seventeen or eighteen. Do you think young people have an easier life now than in the past? Call us and tell us your opinion …

🔊 **8 Skills Test 7&8**
Exercise 1

M: man

M: … Now, this Saturday, there's the football match between Grantly Rovers and the Titchwood Tigers. It's going to be exciting, so come with your whole family. That's Saturday, the fourteenth of June. And that's not all this summer. There's the dance show at the Royal Theatre on the twenty-first of June. Come and watch some great dancers!
July and August are months for music lovers. We begin on the second of July with a concert of classical music. Pianist Wolfgang Schmitt and violinist Marielle Duchamp are going to play Beethoven's music in the concert hall. That's the second of July.
Then on the thirtieth of July, a concert for jazz lovers. Jazz singer Georgia Franklin is going to give a concert in Grantly Park. That's the thirtieth of July, eight o'clock.
Classical music and jazz not for you? Don't worry. Boy band Three Ways are giving a concert on the eleventh of August. Also in the park.
And finally, reggae music by musicians from Jamaica! Don't miss this fantastic concert on the twenty-third of August in the Royal Theatre. Buy your tickets now …

Audio script

🔊 9 Skills Test 7&8
Exercise 2
E: Edith   N: Neil

E: Hi, Neil. What's wrong?

N: Oh, hi, Edith. My Maths teacher is angry with me.

E: Why is she angry?

N: I was late for school this morning – again! But there were a lot of cars on the roads and …

E: There are a lot of cars every morning! Did you come to school by car?

N: Yes, my dad sometimes drives me. There isn't a bus from my house to the school.

E: I came to school on foot this morning and I walked faster than the cars!

N: I know! But you're lucky. You live near the school – and I don't.

E: Hmm. Why didn't you come by bike? It's better than going by car.

N: No, I hate cycling! But I'd like to ride a motorbike … My big brother's got a fantastic new motorbike.

E: Ooh! I love them. I'm going to buy one when I'm eighteen. My parents think they're too dangerous but I'm going to be careful.

N: You know, this town needs an underground! That's the best transport.

E: You're right, but this town is too small for an underground.

🔊 10 Mid-Year Test 1–4
Exercise 7
I: interviewer, girl   A: male actor

I: Welcome to today's programme. Today I'm talking to the famous actor Brandon Murphy. Good morning, Brandon. Your fans would like to know many things about you. Can I ask you some questions?

A: Yes, go ahead!

I: How old are you?

A: I'm twenty-five years old.

I: What's your favourite sport?

A: I like playing football and going windsurfing, but the best sport is karate. I practise every day.

I: What do you like eating?

A: I love fish and I eat it three times a week. With salad.

I: Is there any food you don't like?

A: Ham and sausages! I don't like them at all!

I: What about your hobbies?

A: I'm interested in History and Science and I read books about these subjects. I also like playing chess. It's a cool game!

I: One more question. What are your favourite things?

A: That's easy! My tablet and my mobile phone. I always have them with me.

I: Thank you, Brandon.

🔊 11 End-of-Year Test 1–8
Exercise 7
M: Maria   J: Jules

M: Hi, Jules. It's Maria here.

J: Oh, hi, Maria.

M: I called you last Friday but you weren't at home. Where were you?

J: What time did you call?

M: I think I called at three o'clock.

J: I was at the sports centre. I go there every Friday and I do karate. Then I went to Bobby's house. I was there from four to eight o'clock.

M: Four hours! What did you do there? Did you play computer games?

J: No! I was worried about my Science exam so Bobby helped me study. Then we had dinner. His mum's a fantastic cook.

M: How did you get home? Last Friday was rainy.

J: Bobby's mum took me in her car. It was too late to take a bus.

M: Did you pass your Science exam?

J: Yes, I did!

M: Well done!

J: And I'm going to have a party to celebrate.

M: When?

J: On the twenty-second of February. I'm going to invite everybody in our class.

M: And are you going to invite me?

J: Of course I am! I'm going to write the invitations tonight.

🔊 12 Exam Test 1–4
Part 4
N: narrator   G: girl   M: man

N: Look at the picture. Listen and look. There is one example.

M: And where's that?

G: That's a photo of the summer camp, Grandad. I go there every year with the school.

M: Where are you?

G: I'm not in the photo, but that's my best friend, Clara.

M: The girl reading the book?

G: Yes, Clara's very intelligent. She reads all the time.

N: Can you see the line? This is an example. Now you listen and draw lines.

N: One

M: And who's the boy? He looks cold.

G: Yes, that's Ned. He's funny. He always goes swimming.

M: Do *you* swim in the lake?

G: No! The water's too cold!

N: Two

M: And who are these people?

G: The woman is Mrs Landon. She's our P.E. teacher. She's playing chess with Anton. Anton sits next to me at school. He's a champion chess player.

N: Three

M: Who's that? The girl with the mobile phone?

G: There are two girls with mobile phones …

M: The girl with the long curly hair.

G: Oh, that's Molly. She loves taking photos.

M: Molly's taking a … 'selfie', right? Is 'selfie' the right word?

G: Yes, Grandad! Everyone takes selfies!

N: Four

G: And that's Jess. The girl with the short dark hair.

M: What's she doing?

G: I'm not sure, but I think she's texting a friend.

M: Oh, OK.

N: Five

M: Mm! That sausage looks nice! Who's the boy cooking it?

G: That's Steve. He's always hungry.

M: The dog next to him looks hungry too.

G: That's Mr Baker's dog, Mutt. Mr Baker's our Geography teacher.

N: Six

M: And this girl?

G: Where?

M: Here. With the jumper. She's playing the guitar.

G: That's Becky. She's very talented. She's the best singer in the school.

N: Now listen to Part Four again.

🔊 13 Exam Test 5–8
Part 3
N: narrator   E: Ernie   W: woman

N: Listen and look. There is one example.

W: Ernie, there's a note from your teacher here. Something about a school trip?

E: Oh, yes. Our Science teacher is taking us to a museum.

W: What kind of museum?

E: A natural history museum, you know, with dinosaurs and animals …

N: Can you see the answer? Now you listen and write.

N: One

W: Is that the museum in King Street?

E: No, that's the History Museum. The Natural History Museum is opposite the library.

W: Hmm. That building with the glass walls?

E: That's right.

N: Two

W: And when are you going to go? After the exams?

E: Yes. The exams finish on the eighth of June. That's a Friday. And we're going the next Monday, the eleventh of June.

N: Three

W: Newtown is 60 kilometres away. How are you going to go?

E: The train is expensive so we're going to go with the school bus.

N: Four

E: Can I have some money for the trip?

W: How much money do you need?

E: Twenty pounds?

W: That's a lot! How much is the ticket?

E: It's two pounds for students.

N: Five

W: OK, but why *twenty* pounds?

E: There's a museum shop and I want to buy some posters and books …

W: Twenty pounds is too much. You can have ten pounds.

E: OK, thanks, Mum.

N: Six

W: What time are you going to leave for Newtown?

E: At nine o'clock.

W: And what time are you going to be back at school?

E: At one.

N: Seven

E: Then in the afternoon, I'm going to go to Jenny's house.

W: Why are you going to go there?

E: Because we're going to do a project about the dinosaurs in the museum!

W: Oh, that's nice.

N: Now listen to Part Three again.

Answer key

Placement Test

Exercise 1
A: 1 March 2 excited 3 kitchen 4 milk 5 hall
B: 1 April 2 meat 3 interested 4 canteen 5 garden

Exercise 2
A: 1 headphones 2 an island 3 a screen 4 a volcano 5 a river
B: 1 a screen 2 a river 3 an island 4 headphones 5 a volcano

Exercise 3
A: 1 download 2 do 3 leave 4 buy 5 stay
B: 1 arrive 2 go 3 empty 4 text 5 taking

Exercise 4
A: 1 get 2 opposite 3 expensive 4 restaurant 5 about
B: 1 excited 2 take 3 opposite 4 cheap 5 between

Exercise 5
A: 1 much 2 better 3 am usually 4 any 5 the most intelligent
B: 1 sometimes eat 2 the most difficult 3 much 4 some 5 worse

Exercise 6
A: 1 is studying 2 don't speak 3 'm not watching 4 doesn't brush 5 always go
B: 1 'm not listening 2 usually go 3 don't speak 4 washes 5 is doing

Exercise 7
A: 1 had 2 played 3 went 4 felt 5 didn't meet
B: 1 met 2 bought 3 watched 4 felt 5 didn't go

Exercise 8
A: 1 are 2 is 3 were 4 Did 5 going
B: 1 did 2 going 3 are 4 is 5 was

Exercise 9
A: 1 b 2 a 3 d 4 e 5 c
B: 1 f 2 c 3 b 4 a 5 d

Exercise 10
A: 1 sounds 2 like 3 Here 4 Can 5 Sure
B: 1 sounds 2 borrow 3 problem 4 Excuse 5 straight

Vocabulary Check 1

Exercise 1
A: 1 History 2 French 3 dictionary 4 Music 5 Science 6 Geography 7 map 8 scissors 9 calculator 10 trainers
B: 1 History 2 Music 3 Science 4 Geography 5 map 6 ruler 7 calculator 8 trainers 9 French 10 dictionary

Exercise 2
A: 1 does 2 do 3 plays 4 do 5 plays
B: 1 playing 2 do 3 does 4 play 5 does

Exercise 3
A: 1 a 2 e 3 d 4 b 5 c
B: 1 b 2 a 3 e 4 c 5 d

Vocabulary Check 2

Exercise 1
A: 1 cereal 2 yoghurt 3 orange juice 4 bread 5 cheese 6 biscuits 7 chicken 8 vegetables 9 sausages 10 tomatoes
B: 1 bread 2 cheese 3 fruit 4 biscuits 5 yoghurt 6 cereal 7 meat 8 pasta 9 chicken 10 vegetables

Exercise 2
A: 1 a 2 c 3 e 4 b 5 d
B: 1 b 2 a 3 c 4 e 5 d

Exercise 3
A: 1 carton 2 bar 3 packet 4 jar 5 can
B: 1 jar 2 can 3 bar 4 carton 5 packet

Vocabulary Check 3

Exercise 1
A: 1 talk on the phone 2 mouse 3 text a friend 4 speakers 5 surf the Internet 6 headphones 7 take a selfie 8 screen 9 send an email 10 keyboard
B: 1 surf the Internet 2 screen 3 take a selfie 4 talk on the phone 5 speakers 6 mouse 7 keyboard 8 text a friend 9 send an email 10 headphones

Exercise 2
A: 1 tired 2 bored 3 worried 4 sad 5 angry
B: 1 scared 2 worried 3 tired 4 sad 5 bored

Exercise 3
A: 1 about 2 in 3 about 4 of 5 at
B: 1 about 2 at 3 in 4 of 5 about

Vocabulary Check 4

Exercise 1
A: 1 town 2 beach 3 island 4 desert 5 forest 6 lake 7 river 8 waterfall 9 volcano 10 city
B: 1 city 2 river 3 waterfall 4 sea 5 beach 6 island 7 forest 8 desert 9 lake 10 volcano

Exercise 2
A: 1 safe 2 exciting 3 low 4 cheap 5 difficult
B: 1 high 2 easy 3 expensive 4 safe 5 exciting

Exercise 3
A: 1 e 2 b 3 d 4 a 5 c
B: 1 e 2 b 3 d 4 c 5 a

Vocabulary Check 5

Exercise 1
A: 1 in front of 2 museum 3 between 4 hospital 5 stadium 6 opposite 7 café 8 restaurant 9 library 10 behind
B: 1 in front of 2 stadium 3 museum 4 between 5 hospital 6 opposite 7 café 8 restaurant 9 library 10 behind

Exercise 2
A: 1 b 2 d 3 a 4 e 5 c
B: 1 d 2 e 3 c 4 a 5 b

Exercise 3
A: 1 big 2 dirty 3 modern 4 boring 5 busy
B: 1 modern 2 quiet 3 interesting 4 dirty 5 small

Vocabulary Check 6

Exercise 1
A: 1 farmer 2 police officer 3 artist 4 shop assistant 5 singer 6 pilot 7 nurse 8 chef/cook 9 vet 10 builder
B: 1 singer 2 shop assistant 3 nurse 4 builder 5 vet 6 police officer 7 farmer 8 chef/cook 9 artist 10 pilot

Exercise 2
A: 1 footballer 2 doctor 3 bus driver 4 teacher 5 office worker
B: 1 bus river 2 office worker 3 teacher 4 doctor 5 footballer

Exercise 3
A: 1 make 2 do 3 washes 4 look after 5 empty
B: 1 make 2 walk 3 washes 4 look after 5 empties

Vocabulary Check 7

Exercise 1
A: 1 tram, got off 2 boat, left 3 plane, arrived 4 motorbike 5 foot 6 took, bus
B: 1 foot 2 plane, arrived 3 took, bus 4 motorbike 5 tram, got off 6 boat, left

Exercise 2
A: 1 c 2 a 3 d 4 b 5 e
B: 1 a 2 d 3 b 4 c 5 e

Exercise 3
A: 1 sightseeing 2 hotels 3 souvenirs 4 photos 5 friends
B: 1 restaurant 2 sightseeing 3 friends 4 souvenirs 5 hotel

Vocabulary Check 8

Exercise 1
A: 1 picnic 2 concert 3 sleepover 4 match 5 barbecue 6 fancy dress 7 birthday party 8 talent competition 9 play 10 show
B: 1 sleepover 2 concert 3 play 4 barbecue 5 birthday party 6 show 7 talent competition 8 picnic 9 match 10 fancy dress

Exercise 2
A: 1 the fifteenth of August 2 the twenty-sixth of December 3 the eleventh of November 4 the thirtieth of October 5 the ninth of June
B: 1 the nineteenth of February 2 the twenty-fourth of April 3 the thirty-first of July 4 the eighth of September 5 the fifteenth of November

Exercise 3
A: 1 jazz 2 reggae 3 rap 4 classical 5 rock
B: 1 rap 2 rock 3 jazz 4 reggae 5 classical

Grammar Check 1

Exercise 1
A: 1 washes 2 goes 3 studies 4 like 5 walks
B: 1 brushes 2 cooks 3 do 4 loves 5 studies

Exercise 2
A: 1 You are often late for school. 2 We never go swimming after August. 3 I sometimes play football with my dad. 4 I always ride my bike to school. 5 Jess usually goes to the cinema on Friday.
B: 1 We sometimes take Paul's dog for a walk. 2 My aunt usually visits us at the weekend. 3 I am never late for school. 4 Tim always goes swimming in summer. 5 I often hang out with my friends on Friday.

Exercise 3
A: 1 Yes 2 doesn't 3 we 4 doesn't 5 don't
B: 1 No 2 we 3 doesn't 4 don't 5 Does

Grammar Check 2

Exercise 1
A: 1 b 2 b 3 b 4 b 5 b
B: 1 b 2 a 3 b 4 b 5 b

Exercise 2
A: 1 any 2 some 3 a 4 any 5 any
B: 1 any 2 any 3 any 4 some 5 a

Exercise 3
A: 1 How much 2 How many 3 There are 4 How many 5 a lot of
B: 1 How many 2 How much 3 How many 4 a lot of 5 There's

Grammar Check 3

Exercise 1
A: 1 is studying 2 are talking 3 are chatting 4 are writing 5 am having
B: 1 am having 2 is chatting 3 are studying 4 are making 5 are playing

Answer key

Exercise 2

A: 1 I'm not listening 2 is surfing 3 are running 4 aren't dancing 5 isn't doing

B: 1 is sitting 2 aren't enjoying 3 'm not watching 4 are running 5 isn't doing

Exercise 3

A: 1 am 2 we 3 Is 4 isn't 5 aren't

B: 1 are 2 'm 3 Is 4 isn't 5 they

Grammar Check 4

Exercise 1

A: 1 nicer 2 hotter 3 better 4 more dangerous 5 friendlier

B: 1 hotter 2 more dangerous 3 nicer 4 friendlier 5 worse

Exercise 2

A: 1 Mount Everest is the highest mountain in the group. 2 Dogs are the most intelligent animals in the group. 3 English is the easiest language in the group. 4 Tokyo is the biggest city in the group. 5 Football is the most exciting sport in the group.

B: 1 English is the easiest language in the group. 2 Skiing is the most exciting sport in the group. 3 London is the biggest city in the group. 4 Dogs are the most intelligent animals in the group. 5 Mount Everest is the highest mountain in the group.

Exercise 3

A: 1 more beautiful 2 the best 3 the lowest 4 hungrier 5 the biggest

B: 1 the lowest 2 the biggest 3 more beautiful 4 the best 5 hungrier

Grammar Check 5

Exercise 1

A: 1 were 2 was 3 There was 4 there weren't 5 was

B: 1 was 2 There wasn't 3 there were 4 was 5 were

Exercise 2

A: 1 Was your family at home yesterday? 2 Were there any apples in the garden? 3 Where was Kevin last night? 4 Was there a party at school yesterday? 5 Was Maria at the theatre last night?

B: 1 Where was Peter last night? 2 Was Diana at the restaurant last week? 3 Was your family at home last night? 4 Was there a party in the street yesterday? 5 Were there any flowers in the garden?

Exercise 3

A: 1 Yes, they were. 2 Yes, it was. 3 Yes, there was. 4 No, it wasn't. 5 No, there weren't.

B: 1 No, there wasn't. 2 Yes, there were. 3 No, it wasn't. 4 Yes, it was. 5 No, they weren't.

Grammar Check 6

Exercise 1

A: 1 played 2 stopped 3 watched 4 stayed 5 tried

B: 1 tried 2 walked 3 played 4 stopped 5 tidied

Exercise 2

A: 1 went 2 met 3 made 4 came 5 had

B: 1 made 2 had 3 came 4 went 5 met

Exercise 3

A: 1 drank 2 ate 3 took 4 met 5 felt

B: 1 had 2 took 3 met 4 felt 5 drank

Grammar Check 7

Exercise 1

A: 1 didn't stop 2 didn't study 3 didn't do 4 didn't make 5 didn't eat

B: 1 didn't buy 2 didn't do 3 didn't stop 4 didn't drink 5 didn't text

Exercise 2

A: 1 Did you sleep 2 Did Mr Fey stay 3 Did their mum drink 4 Did they take 5 Did you have

B: 1 Did you eat 2 Did Jenny have 3 Did his mum watch 4 Did the cat sleep 5 Did Dad take

Exercise 3

A: 1 No, she didn't. 2 Yes, they did. 3 No, you didn't. 4 Yes, it did. 5 No, he didn't.

B: 1 No, he didn't. 2 Yes, you did. 3 No, it didn't. 4 Yes, they did. 5 No, we didn't.

Grammar Check 8

Exercise 1

A: 1 Are you and Jack going to buy 2 is going to show 3 aren't going to play 4 am going to watch 5 Is your uncle going to visit

B: 1 aren't going to go 2 Are you going to watch 3 isn't going to cook 4 'm going to visit 5 Are you and I going to meet

Exercise 2

A: 1 study 2 we 3 to 4 No 5 Are

B: 1 to 2 Yes 3 blow 4 aren't 5 Is

Exercise 3

A: 1 Can you play the guitar? 2 Has Jack got a pet rabbit? 3 Does Morag do karate at the weekend? 4 Are the children eating apples? 5 Did we sleep in a tent in summer?

B: 1 Does Piotr go sailing at the weekend? 2 Did we wear costumes to the party? 3 Can Gemma take great photos? 4 Are Granny and Grandad sitting in the garden? 5 Have the children got new laptops?

Language Test
Get started!

Exercise 1

A: 1 shower 2 wardrobe 3 shelves 4 fridge 5 next to

B: 1 shelves 2 next to 3 fridge 4 wardrobe 5 shower

Exercise 2

A: 1 American 2 Trainers 3 Clever 4 France 5 Summer

B: 1 American 2 Trousers 3 Helpful 4 France 5 Autumn

Exercise 3

A: 1 c 2 e 3 a 4 d 5 b

B: 1 c 2 a 3 b 4 d 5 e

Exercise 4

A: 1 a 2 c 3 c 4 c 5 b

B: 1 c 2 a 3 a 4 c 5 c

Exercise 5

A: 1 Sean's 2 our 3 its 4 Barbara 5 Their

B: 1 its 2 Their 3 Zoe 4 our 5 Paul's

Exercise 6

A: 1 got 2 are 3 have 4 can 5 aren't

B: 1 got 2 are 3 have 4 can't 5 are

Language Test 1

Exercise 1

A: 1 dictionary 2 Geography 3 maps 4 calculator 5 Science 6 play 7 do

B: 1 dictionary 2 calculator 3 History 4 Geography 5 maps 6 do 7 play

Exercise 2

A: 1 hall 2 canteen 3 staff room 4 gym

B: 1 staff room 2 playground 3 library 4 canteen

Exercise 3

A: 1 We are never late for Music lessons. 2 Lucille and Jon sometimes walk to school. 3 You usually have lunch at home. 4 I often hang out with my friends.

B: 1 Ken never meets his friends in the park. 2 The students usually have lunch at home. 3 You are sometimes late for school. 4 My friends often ride their bikes to school.

Exercise 4

A: 1 has 2 does 3 doesn't watch 4 don't go 5 work

B: 1 does 2 watches 3 doesn't play 4 work 5 don't go

Exercise 5

A: 1 Yes 2 Does 3 Do 4 they 5 What

B: 1 No 2 Do 3 we 4 What 5 Does

Exercise 6

A: 1 spell that/it 2 are you 3 you live 4 email address 5 phone number

B: 1 spell that/it 2 are you 3 you live 4 email address 5 phone number

Language Test 2

Exercise 1

A: 1 pancakes 2 milk 3 pasta 4 yoghurt

B: 1 pasta 2 pancakes 3 yoghurt 4 milk

Exercise 2

A: 1 rice 2 sausages 3 chips 4 strawberries 5 cheese 6 sugar

B: 1 chips 2 rice 3 sausages 4 cheese 5 strawberries 6 sugar

Exercise 3

A: 1 cans 2 bottle 3 jar 4 carton

B: 1 bar 2 jar 3 bottle 4 cans

Exercise 4

A: 1 – 2 an 3 – 4 – 5 a

B: 1 an 2 – 3 – 4 – 5 a

Exercise 5

A: 1 many 2 a 3 any 4 some 5 much 6 a lot

B: 1 much 2 a lot 3 some 4 any 5 any 6 many

Exercise 6

A: 1 Are you ready to order? What would you like? 2 Can I have the pancakes, please? 3 And would you like anything to drink? 4 Yes, please. I'd like a glass of cola, please. 5 Anything else? 6 No, thank you.

B: 1 Are you ready to order? What would you like? 2 Can I have a pizza, please? 3 And would you like anything to drink? 4 Yes, please. I'd like a glass of juice, please. 5 Anything else? 6 No, thank you.

Language Test 3

Exercise 1

A: 1 talk 2 tablet 3 download 4 headphones 5 send 6 text 7 online

B: 1 surf 2 laptop 3 download 4 headphones 5 send 6 text 7 chat

Exercise 2

A: 1 good 2 interested 3 scared 4 tired 5 worried

B: 1 scared 2 worried 3 interested 4 good 5 tired

Exercise 3

A: 1 aren't watching 2 's writing 3 's listening 4 am I doing 5 'm surfing

Answer key

B: 1 's doing   2 're talking   3 isn't watching   4 's singing   5 are you doing

Exercise 4
A: 1 I'm not   2 he/she is   3 we aren't   4 they are
B: 1 she isn't   2 we are   3 he is   4 they aren't

Exercise 5
A: 1 What is Roxanne driving?   2 Why are you going to bed?   3 Are the cats are sleeping on the carpet?   4 What are the students reading?
B: 1 Are the teachers sitting in the staff room?   2 What is Louisa drinking?   3 Why are Kate and you going home?   4 Where are the little girls playing?

Exercise 6
A: 1 Fine   2 speak   3 please   4 Hang   5 soon
B: 1 fine   2 speak   3 please   4 Just   5 later

Language Test 4

Exercise 1
A: 1 city   2 forest   3 desert   4 beach   5 river   6 island   7 volcano
B: 1 desert   2 river   3 volcano   4 city   5 beach   6 island   7 forest

Exercise 2
A: 1 beautiful   2 kind   3 expensive   4 boring   5 low
B: 1 low   2 beautiful   3 exciting   4 cheap   5 kind

Exercise 3
A: 1 is higher than   2 are bigger than   3 is better than   4 are more dangerous than   5 is easier than
B: 1 is worse than   2 is more expensive than   3 are cuter than   4 are faster than   5 is easier than

Exercise 4
A: 1 the curliest   2 the hottest   3 the best   4 the most boring
B: 1 the most boring   2 the curliest   3 the best   4 the hottest

Exercise 5
A: 1 the   2 more   3 most   4 than
B: 1 than   2 the   3 most   4 more

Exercise 6
A: 1 about   2 of   3 think   4 opinion   5 right
B: 1 you   2 favourite   3 think   4 in   5 right

Language Test 5

Exercise 1
A: 1 post office   2 hotel   3 swimming pool   4 bank   5 hospital   6 restaurant   7 theatre
B: 1 hospital   2 bank   3 library   4 restaurant   5 theatre   6 hotel   7 post office

Exercise 2
A: 1 next to   2 between   3 opposite   4 Behind
B: 1 between   2 next to   3 opposite   4 behind

Exercise 3
A: 1 clean   2 modern   3 quiet   4 interesting
B: 1 dirty   2 modern   3 busy   4 boring

Exercise 4
A: 1 weren't   2 was   3 were   4 weren't   5 wasn't
B: 1 were   2 was   3 weren't   4 were   5 wasn't

Exercise 5
A: 1 Yes   2 weren't   3 there   4 wasn't   5 was
B: 1 No   2 were   3 there   4 was   5 wasn't

Exercise 6
A: 1 on   2 far   3 straight   4 past   5 right
B: 1 on   2 far   3 straight   4 past   5 left

Language Test 6

Exercise 1
A: 1 artist   2 pilot   3 chef/cook   4 builder   5 vet
B: 1 chef/cook   2 vet   3 builder   4 pilot   5 artist

Exercise 2
A: 1 singer   2 office worker   3 nurse   4 shop assistant
B: 1 nurse   2 singer   3 shop assistant   4 office worker

Exercise 3
A: 1 a   2 c   3 b   4 c
B: 1 c   2 c   3 a   4 b

Exercise 4
A: 1 arrived   2 played   3 made   4 wanted   5 stopped   6 went
B: 1 went   2 listened   3 made   4 wanted   5 stopped   6 walked

Exercise 5
A: 1 took   2 met   3 lived   4 tried   5 came   6 had
B: 1 asked   2 had   3 ate   4 took   5 came   6 tried

Exercise 6
A: 1 Sure   2 if   3 fine   4 please   5 sorry
B: 1 all   2 if   3 problem   4 please   5 sorry

Language Test 7

Exercise 1
A: 1 on   2 arrive   3 takes   4 leaves   5 underground   6 motorbike
B: 1 on   2 take   3 leave   4 bus   5 arrive   6 motorbike

Exercise 2
A: 1 sightseeing   2 hotel   3 sunglasses   4 sleeping bags   5 suitcase   6 souvenirs
B: 1 sightseeing   2 hotel   3 sleeping bags   4 souvenirs   5 suitcase   6 sunglasses

Exercise 3
A: 1 didn't take   2 didn't watch   3 didn't surf   4 didn't use   5 had
B: 1 didn't text   2 didn't chat   3 didn't watch   4 didn't use   5 had

Exercise 4
A: 1 Did he eat   2 he did   3 Did they cook   4 they didn't
B: 1 Did she tidy   2 she did   3 Did they eat   4 they didn't

Exercise 5
A: 1 Where did you go?   2 How did you travel there?   3 Did you see Granada?   4 When did you come home?
B: 1 Where did you travel?   2 How did you go there?   3 Did you see the Rhine?   4 When did you come home?

Exercise 6
A: 1 I'd like a ticket to Manchester, please.   2 Here you are.   3 How much is it?   4 It's seventy-five pounds, please.   5 What time does the train leave?   6 At ten minutes to eight.   7 Thanks.
B: 1 I'd like a ticket to Bristol, please.   2 Here you are.   3 How much is it?   4 It's thirty pounds fifty, please.   5 What time does the train leave?   6 At three minutes past five.   7 Thanks.

Language Test 8

Exercise 1
A: 1 sleepover   2 talent competition   3 barbecue   4 play   5 picnic   6 fancy dress party
B: 1 barbecue   2 picnic   3 play   4 talent competition   5 fancy dress party   6 sleepover

Exercise 2
A: 1 reggae   2 the fifteenth of January   3 classical   4 the twenty-seventh of August   5 the thirty-first of October   6 jazz
B: 1 classical   2 the nineteenth of June   3 the thirteenth of September   4 jazz   5 reggae   6 the twenty-second of November

Exercise 3
A: 1 are going to get up   2 is going to invite   3 are going to go   4 aren't going to stay
B: 1 are going to do   2 is going to buy   3 are going to invite   4 aren't going to go

Exercise 4
A: 1 I'm   2 Is   3 to   4 are
B: 1 am   2 are   3 Is   4 going

Exercise 5
A: 1 Have you got an invitation to the party?   2 When does the football match start?   3 Why are they running?   4 Where did Joshua go last summer?   5 How many new friends did you make on holiday?

B: 1 How does Jasper go to school?   2 How many computer games have you got?   3 What did Melissa make yesterday?   4 Where are the children playing?   5 Why did you go to bed early?

Exercise 6
A: 1 tickets   2 Would   3 sounds   4 meet   5 Let's
B: 1 like   2 sounds   3 I'd   4 shall   5 Let's

Skills Test 1-2

Exercise 1
A: 1 d   2 c   3 a   4 f   5 b
B: 1 f   2 e   3 d   4 a   5 c

Exercise 2
A: 1 eggs   2 pasta   3 fruit   4 salad   5 pancakes
B: 1 eggs   2 tomatoes   3 cheese   4 chicken   5 strawberries

Exercise 3
A: 1 a   2 b   3 c   4 a   5 b
B: 1 a   2 b   3 c   4 c   5 b

Exercise 4
A: 1 T   2 T   3 F   4 T   5 F
B: 1 T   2 F   3 F   4 F   5 T

Exercise 5
A: 1 don't   2 eggs   3 carton   4 bar   5 sugar
B: 1 lot   2 eggs   3 carton   4 is   5 sugar

Exercise 6
Model text

On school days I get up at seven o'clock. I usually have cereal and some orange juice for breakfast. Lessons begin at half past eight. My favourite subjects are Maths and English but I also like History and Music. I always have lunch in the canteen at school. I usually have pasta or fish and vegetables. Lessons finish at three o'clock and then I go home.

Skills Test 3-4

Exercise 1
Mum – woman sitting at table studying
Dennis – boy sitting on sofa watching TV
Dad – man sitting in armchair, listening to music through headphones
Lawrence – boy sitting on sofa and texting on mobile phone
Sabina – girl lying on carpet reading
Muppet – cat playing with mouse

Exercise 2
A: 1 c   2 b   3 a   4 d   5 e
B: 1 c   2 e   3 b   4 a   5 d

Answer key

Exercise 3
A: 1 e 2 g 3 a 4 d 5 c
B: 1 a 2 f 3 c 4 b 5 e

Exercise 4
A: 1 You can go swimming, windsurfing and sailing. 2 The Golo river/It's 90 kilometres long. 3 She doesn't like swimming in the lake because the water is cold. 4 He thinks/says it's too dangerous. 5 They're eating sausages and cheese.
B: 1 She's swimming in a lake. 2 (Joy's mum's says) it's better to swim in the sea. 3 You can walk, go mountain biking and go rock climbing. 4 It's next to the sea. 5 They're sitting under an umbrella (in Ajaccio).

Exercise 5
A: 1 tablet 2 chat 3 selfies 4 interested 5 downloads
B: 1 tablet 2 chat 3 selfies 4 interested 5 downloads

Exercise 6
Model text

My friend Stella is tall with fair hair and blue eyes. I'm taller than Stella and I've got dark hair and green eyes. We like playing computer games and running. Stella is interested in History but I'm not. I'm interested in Science. We're both good at Music but I'm better. Stella and her family usually go to the mountains in summer. My family and I go to the beach.

Skills Test 5–6
Exercise 1
A: 1 a 2 c 3 b 4 b 5 a
B: 1 c 2 b 3 c 4 a 5 b

Exercise 2
A: 1 dishes 2 younger 3 vegetable 4 helped 5 animals
B: 1 floors 2 children 3 fathers 4 fix 5 looked

Exercise 3
A: 1 Where's the Science Museum? 2 Is it far from here? 3 Can we walk there? 3 How can we get to Dover Street? 5 Can I borrow your pen, please?
B: 1 Where's the History Museum? 2 Is it far from here? 3 Can we walk there? 4 How can we get to Suffolk Street? 5 Can I borrow your pen, please?

Exercise 4
A: 1 T 2 F 3 DS 4 DS 5 T
B: 1 DS 2 T 3 F 4 DS 5 F

Exercise 5
A: 1 chef 2 restaurant 3 nurse 4 looks 5 officer
B: 1 assistant 2 hospital 3 looks 4 nurse 5 police

Exercise 6
Model text

Last Sunday, we went to Chester. My grandparents live there and we wanted to see them. First, we had lunch and talked to Granny and Grandpa. Then Dad took us to Chester Zoo. There were a lot of interesting animals there but the elephants were my favourite! They're very intelligent. After that, we went to a restaurant and had dinner. We arrived home late. I was tired but very happy.

Skills Test 7–8
Exercise 1
A: 1 no 2 yes 3 no 4 yes 5 no
B: 1 yes 2 yes 3 no 4 yes 5 no

Exercise 2
A: 1 By car. 2 No, there isn't. 3 On foot./She walked. 4 They're (too) dangerous. 5 (The) underground.
B: 1 His dad/father. 2 Near the school. 3 He hates cycling. 4 A (fantastic) (new) motorbike. 5 (An) underground.

Exercise 3
A: 1 f 2 g 3 a 4 d 5 c
B: 1 b 2 a 3 e 4 c 5 g

Exercise 4
A: 1 lunch time 2 sightseeing 3 next to 4 a lot of 5 camera
B: 1 hungry 2 to town 3 swimming pool 4 people 5 took some photos

Exercise 5
A: 1 tents 2 took 3 barbecue 4 drank 5 better
B: 1 backpacks 2 took 3 ate 4 drank 5 exciting

Exercise 6
Model text

Hi Alistair,
I'm having a lovely time in Austria with my family. There's snow on the mountains but it's sunny. We're staying in a small hotel.
Yesterday we went skiing and I had a lot of fun. Then we had dinner at a restaurant.
Tomorrow we're going to go to Innsbruck. Mum wants to do some shopping and we're going to meet our Austrian friends there.
See you soon!
Neville

Mid-Year Test
Exercise 1
A: 1 coat 2 shower 3 carton 4 flour 5 city
B: 1 fridge 2 shirt 3 jar 4 butter 5 town

Exercise 2
A: 1 drums 2 do 3 headphones 4 download 5 about
B: 1 the drums 2 do 3 speakers 4 download 5 dangerous

Exercise 3
A: 1 expensive 2 pretty 3 angry 4 kind 5 tired
B: 1 pretty 2 expensive 3 cheaper 4 tired 5 angry

Exercise 4
A: 1 doesn't like 2 usually listens 3 do 4 don't go 5 do you spend
B: 1 usually plays 2 doesn't like 3 do 4 don't have 5 do you do

Exercise 5
A: 1 aren't swimming 2 are taking 3 is running 4 isn't wearing 5 are Mabel and Darren doing
B: 1 are taking 2 isn't looking 3 is reading 4 aren't swimming 5 are Lacey and Joe going

Exercise 6
A: 1 any 2 bigger 3 than 4 much 5 most
B: 1 than 2 most 3 any 4 many 5 better

Exercise 7
A: 1 karate 2 salad 3 ham 4 Science 5 chess 6 tablet
B: 1 windsurfing 2 fish 3 sausages 4 History 5 chess 6 phone

Exercise 8
A: 1 c 2 a 3 i 4 f 5 b 6 g 7 h 8 d
B: 1 h 2 i 3 f 4 c 5 a 6 e 7 b 8 g

Exercise 9
A: 1 T 2 F 3 DS 4 T 5 F 6 DS
B: 1 T 2 F 3 DS 4 T 5 F 6 DS

End-of-Year Test
Exercise 1
A: 1 milk 2 maps 3 builder 4 torch 5 museum
B: 1 water 2 scissors 3 pilot 4 tram 5 hotel

Exercise 2
A: 1 does 2 leaves 3 officer 4 after 5 dirty
B: 1 assistant 2 clean 3 makes 4 leaves 5 after

Exercise 3
A: 1 desert 2 visit 3 concerts 4 surf 5 easy
B: 1 forest 2 plays 3 visit 4 online 5 difficult

Exercise 4
A: 1 many 2 prettier 3 last 4 most 5 any
B: 1 most 2 last 3 some 4 much 5 higher

Exercise 5
A: 1 are enjoying 2 goes 3 had 4 ate 5 aren't going to do
B: 1 are enjoying 2 goes 3 met 4 had 5 aren't going to do

Exercise 6
A: 1 Does Ricky/he cook lunch every day? 2 Where were you yesterday? 3 Did your team win the match? 4 What did you watch on TV last night? 5 Are you going to study for the English test tomorrow?
B: 1 Does Priscilla/she cook dinner every evening? 2 What did you watch on TV last night? 3 Where were you last Saturday? 4 Did your team win the match? 5 Are you going to study for the Maths test tomorrow?

Exercise 7
A: 1 (at) /three o'clock 2 karate 3 four/4 4 his Science exam 5 by car / Bobby's mum took him in the car 6 22nd February/the twenty-second of February
B: 1 at the sports centre 2 (at) four o'clock 3 his Science exam 4 Bobby's mum (took him). 5 22nd February/the twenty-second of February 6 tonight

Exercise 8
A: 1 a 2 b 3 b 4 a 5 b 6 a 7 b 8 b
B: 1 b 2 a 3 a 4 b 5 a 6 b 7 a 8 b

Exercise 9
A: 1 F 2 T 3 DS 4 T 5 DS 6 F
B: 1 F 2 F 3 DS 4 T 5 DS 6 T

Exam Test 1–4
Part 1
1 a desert 2 potatoes 3 a dictionary 4 a volcano 5 a bottle 6 a mouse

Part 2
1 than 2 often think 3 but 4 don't 5 spending 6 a lot of

Part 3
1 headphones 2 the guitar 3 on a wall 4 a dress /an expensive dress
Possible answers: 5, 6
The girl is talking on her mobile phone.
The man in the car is angry.
The woman is wearing a coat.
The dress in the shop is expensive.